# The Productive Little Citizens

Developing an Emotionally Supportive Community

Sheryl L. Brown, LFMT, CCDIS

*Opulence Publishing*

## Opulence Publishing

Cumming, GA 30041

www.superfunshow.com

Printed in the United States of America

ISBN 978-0-9896254-3-2

# Dedication

This book is lovingly dedicated to all the children who are in need of an emotionally supportive community while developing into productive little citizens.

# Foreword

*The Productive Little Citizens* serves as a blueprint for creating a community of students who are connected to the learning process. As a school psychologist, I often see the direct effects of social maladjustment on a student's ability to acquire curriculum content. Through the acquisition of "people-centered" leadership skills, an educator can ensure that each child will be validated while the teacher still achieves his or her goals and objectives.

Readers will gain an awareness of a child's "mental movie" as a point of reference for effective intervention to produce engaged learners. Sheryl Brown presents relevant methodology in a manner that can be applied to all socioeconomic and cultural backgrounds. *The Productive Little Citizens* is applicable to the new teacher, seasoned teacher, and school-wide educational support teams. In addition, it provides social constructs to support the development of Positive Behavior Intervention and Supports (PBIS). This book is a must-have for every educator's library.

Gina Gordon Lopez
School Psychologist/Licensed Educational Psychologist
Bakersfield City School District (K-8)

# Contents

# Preface

Have you ever once imagined your classroom and/or your home environment as being a community, rather than just a classroom or home? Have you ever considered the children you either teach or raise as being little citizens, rather than just mere students or dependents? The fact of the matter is educators and parents alike have never really been challenged to think beyond traditional beliefs, which have historically defined our educational system (at home or school) as being an institutional setting. The word institution in and of itself sounds so formal, insensitive, impersonal, and, in some ways, mechanical that one could possibly question if our existing institutional school setting is fully equipped to properly and effectively address the emotional needs of today's children—especially in a world where things are becoming more complex and challenging each day.

Increasing divorce rates; child abuse, abandonment, and neglect; economic crises; wars and rumors of war; environmental catastrophes; protests; political uproars; loss of loved ones; domestic violence; epidemics; and parental drug addictions; the list of societal ills could go on and on. Sadly, these issues have taken root in the minds of our children. Today's children are feeling the brunt of our societal woes to the point that their emotional wellbeing is being jeopardized. The majority of the behavior problems displayed by children at home and/or school are immediately treated with prescription medications, which are designed only to get to the surface of the problem. Let the truth be told: children are desperately trying to communicate to us their frustrations, fears, anger, disappointments, confusion, hurts, and/or concerns. But are we listening? They are in need of someone to take the time out of his or her busy schedule and come into their little world and look beyond their behavior to interpret what they are really trying to convey through their emotions.

My desire is to persuade you not only to adopt the ideology behind having an emotionally supportive community, but also to implement diligently the information introduced in each chapter. By doing so, you will witness right before your eyes children transforming into productive little citizens. Remember, children only want to be heard, but we must understand they often communicate through their emotions, rather than their words.

Sheryl L. Brown

*Emotions are themes of one's thoughts, while feelings are the actors of one's emotions.*

# We All Have Them: Emotions

### Emotions vs. Feelings

Emotions are not given to a selected few; rather, emotions are part of every human's psychological makeup. An emotion (i.e., fear, joy, shame, etc.) is best described as being a byproduct of one's thoughts that results from an actual experience (past or present), event, opinion, and/or an imaginary episode. Emotions are what I call the "themes" of an individual's thoughts or mental state and are expressed through a person's feelings (i.e., happy, sad, upset, etc.). Emotions are specifically designed to move an individual in the direction that reflects the thought currently pondered.

In essence, an emotion is a mental state of being, and a feeling is a physical state of being. An emotion is the theme of a thought, and a feeling is a physical reaction to the emotion. Both are designed to bring life and meaning to the thought so that the individual can be cognizant of what he or she is experiencing physically. Now, let me add one more twist to all of this: an individual's behavior (also referred to as physical actions), such as hitting and crying, is the tangible manifestation of one's feelings. In other words, feelings are the channels in which one's emotions can be visibly seen. Feelings are like stage actors that dramatize, through an individual's physical actions, the emotions (the themes) that are triggered by a thought.

Let me put this together with an illustration. Lately, Adam has been reflecting on the loss of his pet dog Mikko, who was recently put to sleep. Adam is feeling quite sad and shows no interest when asked by his mother if he wants to go outside and play. Adam's thoughts are constantly reminding him of what he is currently experiencing, namely, missing his dog Mikko. The emotion or "theme" that is his being triggered by Adam's thought is sadness. This "theme," sadness, is now being outwardly expressed through his physical actions, such as not wanting to go outside to play. So an emotion can only be seen through an accompanying feeling, and a feeling (or feelings) can only be observed through one's behavior.

*Emotions are not given to a selected few; rather, emotions are part of every human's psychological makeup.*

I know what I have just described to you, or rather my interpretation of how the mind, emotions, and feelings interplay with each other, may sound somewhat complex, but the takeaway is this: all children rely heavily on their emotions and feelings to communicate to you what they are experiencing in their little, but real, world.

I will go into further details in this book regarding the importance of being sensitive to the emotions children present, and I will discuss how to effectively interpret these emotions—especially when the behavior being displayed is of concern. So become familiar with the terminologies presented to you in this chapter, and be cognizant of how your mind, emotions, and feelings attempt to govern your life and that of your little citizens.

## Emotions, What They Are and Are Not

Even though emotions are psychologically innate and play a significant role in assisting us as humans in deciphering our reality, emotions, like many things in life, have their proper place. That is, our emotions were not designed to dominate our life, but rather to make us aware of life experiences. With that being said, let's briefly look at what emotions are and are not.

1. Emotions do provide a means to express and acknowledge one's thoughts in a healthy way. If all we had were thoughts, but no way to outwardly express them, we would have persistent, heavy thoughts weighing on our minds, which would be detrimental to our health. According to research by Aletha Solter, crying releases emotions. This release not only has the ability to remove toxins from the body, but it also decreases tension. It was also noted that it is necessary for children to communicate their painful feelings through crying in an effort to heal properly from distressing experiences (Solter,1989).

2. Our emotions are the basis of our belief system. Our emotions are also constantly changing. New themes and new emotions are continuously making guest appearances throughout the day, based on an actual experience or the memory of a past event. As a result, we can be up one moment and down another; we can be confident one moment and uncertain the next. Our emotions can be quite wishy-washy and should never be viewed as the sum total of our belief system.

3. Emotions are not to be used to justify our behavior, especially

when an inappropriate behavior is involved. As stated earlier, emotions are themes that describe or define our mental state. Some of the thoughts we have throughout the day might be unusual, thereby triggering emotions and feelings that will take us out of character if acted upon. For example, while waiting in line to pay for his groceries, a gentleman noticed an elderly lady in front of him with a sizeable amount of items. A crazy thought came across his mind to push the lady down and get in front of her in line. The emotions and feelings that were stimulating this gentleman's thoughts could not excuse his behavior if acted upon. Ultimately, he had the right to either refuse or succumb to the mental suggestions that were challenging his character and behavior. All he could do was laugh because, in actuality, he holds high regard for women of all ages.

*Your emotions are designed to assist you in connecting with others from the standpoint that they allow you to look beyond self and be more empathetic towards those with whom you come in contact during your life journey.*

4. Emotions should not be the authority by which decisions are made. Your emotions do not consider all the facts that are needed to make a decision. Your ability to make quality decisions should be greater than how you feel.

5. Your emotions are designed to assist you in connecting with others from the standpoint that they allow you to look beyond self and be more empathetic towards those with whom you come in contact during your life journey.

# Reflections

# Reflections

# *Reflections*

# Chapter 2

## Being the Thermostat of Your Community

During the introduction, I challenged you, the parent and/or educator, to start visualizing your classroom or home environment as a community. The information you will receive from here on out will be helpful in establishing a strong community that fosters emotional support and causes your little citizens to successfully thrive under your leadership. So, right now make up your mind that your role as a leader should not be minimized by anyone, not even by you. Constantly remind yourself that you play a vital role in the lives of the children you oversee on a daily basis. Remember, it is an honor to impact the lives of your children in order for them to become productive little citizens.

Being a leader is a privilege, honor, and a responsibility all wrapped up in one. However, in order to adequately fill the shoes of a leader, you must first be in tune with who *you* are, and that includes your emotional state of being. Are you moody, depressed, or anxious? Are your emotions in control of you? Or, are you in control of your emotions?

You might say, "Oh, Sheryl, we do not have any control over our emotions!" Contrary to popular belief, yes you do! Your emotions are only themes that are regulated by your thoughts, and they can be changed or replaced with another thought in a matter of seconds. In other words, your thoughts will determine the emotions that are activated. It is essential for you to be in control so that you will not find yourself vulnerable to your emotions, especially when others are depending on you for emotional stability.

Let me make something clear before proceeding any further, you are not going to be emotionally "perfect" 24/7, simply because life is famous for throwing unexpected curve balls (challenges) your way that can catch you off guard. But as long as you are capable and willing to transition from a not-so-pleasant emotional state to a more pleasant one for the sake of your little citizens, you are well on your way to having a productive community.

*In order to adequately fill the shoes of a leader, you must first be in tune with who you are, and that includes your emotional state of being.*

Ladies, I find this to be particularly true for us because we must wear a lot of hats (i.e., educator, counselor, liaison, mother, nurturer, chef, wife, etc.), even when we do not feel like it. When I was having a very challenging time in my life, my sister Brenda made one statement that made a lasting impression. She said, "Sister, if you keep a smile on your face, even when things seem unbearable, people will never know what you are going through." Wow! What a word! I have found this priceless advice, even today, to be so true. Ladies and gentlemen, parents and educators, your emotional and mental state has a significant impact over the emotional vibe of the community you lead.

*I'll never forget the story a lead teacher in Louisiana told about her assistant teacher who was emotionally abused as a child. The emotionally hurt individual never received counseling to address her childhood trauma; as a result, she carried her emotional pain into her classroom community. Not aware of her behavior, she became emotionally abusive to the little citizens, even to the point that one little boy dreaded coming to school. Every day, he would peek inside the classroom to see if the assistant teacher was present. He would leave one foot outside of the classroom and would ask, "Is she here yet?" He was only three but was very fearful and uncomfortable with the emotional climate of his community.*

As the leader of your community, the demeanor you choose to represent your emotional and mental state will definitely have an influence on the overall emotional climate of the community. So being up one day and down another is not an option, especially when your little citizens are depending on you for emotional support. Make this statement of declaration each day before you walk into your community: "I am the thermostat for my community!"

## Relevance of Being the Thermostat of Your Community

So with all that being said, the first key element to developing an emotionally supportive community is taking ownership of your emotions and making the necessary adjustments in order to be an effective thermostat for your community. Let's briefly examine the importance of being a steady thermostat who provides stable emotional support for your little citizens.

1. You must generate positive peer relationships amongst the citizens within the community. The community is only as strong as its strongest link, the leader. Children's ability to get along with each other is strongly influenced by the leader, who must constantly interject harmony into her community, through respect, interactive activities which stimulate the citizens to depend on each other, and/or through demonstrating sensitivity to the feelings of others.

2. The little citizens emotionally "feed" off of you. I really cannot emphasize it enough that you are the thermostat for your com-

munity, whether at home or school. You set the temperature by the attitude you choose to embrace, which, in turn, shapes the behavior you display in front of the children. Your emotions and feelings are constantly being expressed through your behavior. What you think—not only about yourself, but also about the little citizens under your watch—will play a big part when it comes to determining if your community will flourish or wither.

3.  A community's temperature that is constantly fueled by love, laughter, sensitivity, acceptance, and guidance creates a positive atmosphere. Thus, when a child is emotionally distressed, the temperature in the community is prepared to take the brunt of the child's frustration, anger, and/or sadness. The community leader is prepared to help him or her recover from whatever caused him to be emotionally distressed. Once the issue has been resolved, the little citizen is encouraged to flow right back into his community and function as normal. **Note:** A child who is emotionally `distressed should never change the setting of the community's thermostat; rather, his emotional concerns must be properly attended to so that he feels comfortable to blend back into the community and engage accordingly.

4.  Living an exemplary life is an ongoing commitment from the standpoint that those who are under your leadership are endlessly drawing from your words of encouragement and affection and, yes, even from your emotional stability. Children are experts in their own right when it comes to having a keen sense of knowing when something is not right. They may not be able to articulate through words what is wrong, but children are definitely able to express with a hug or smile or by simply saying, "I love you," to make you aware that they are emotionally connected to you at that moment. When you exemplify emotional stability, you are teaching your citizens, through your attitude and behavior, how to gauge their own emotions in a healthy way.

5. A stable atmosphere creates a focus-minded environment where the little citizens are able to effectively focus on fulfilling the goals and completing the assignments of the community. When the leader of the community is diligent in making sure the positive atmosphere is the standard, or norm, for the community, the children become acclimated to the atmosphere; therefore, they are able to direct their attention appropriately and engage in the affairs of the community. I had an opportunity to observe an early childhood educator create a positive atmosphere in which she and her little citizens would greet each other first thing in the morning. She would play joyful music each morning that promoted cooperation among peers. This educator strategically created a positive atmosphere first thing in the morning so that the mindset of her little citizens would be fresh and ready to learn and engage in the curriculum and activities planned for the day. In other words, this educator was presenting the type of emotions and/or feelings she wanted her little citizens to gravitate to, for the sake of their well-being and for having a productive day.

6. The little citizens can flourish and grow within the well-regulated community. I don't know about you, but when the temperature is just right in our home, everyone is comfortable and can function accordingly. In the same manner, when the thermostat (you) is emotionally stable, the temperature is comfortable in the community so that the little citizen can flourish and grow physically, mentally, emotionally, socially, and academically. In other words, children need to feel comfortable in growing and exploring who they are.

I would like to commend my parents for always providing for my brother and me an emotionally supportive community at home so that we could flourish and grow into productive citizens. My parents were cognizant of not bringing their personal problems to our attention; rather, they guarded us from certain issues so that we could enjoy our childhood. Anyhow, what could we have done as children to resolve any emotional issues my parents were experiencing?

Leaders, always remember the following: You are the thermostat for your community. Your attitude and demeanor sets the temperature, which becomes the baseline for the community.

# Reflections

# Reflections

# *Reflections*

*A people-centered leader is always looking beyond self in order to see the needs of others.*

## Self-Centered Leader
## vs. People-Centered Leader

Another key to developing an emotionally supportive community for your little citizens is being a people-centered leader, rather than a self-centered leader. The leadership style you decide to adopt will determine the strength and efficiency of your community. Whether the community is your home or your classroom, you will find children are always going to be in need of YOU, in need of your hugs, your approval, your validation, your support, your love, your protection, your guidance, and your laughter. Truly, the needs go on and on. The bottom line is this: you are in high demand as a leader, so you must be comfortable with sharing yourself with others.

*I recall a story about a teacher who had a difficult time giving and receiving hugs from her little citizens. She would distance herself emotionally from her students to the point that the members of the community would seek the emotional support they needed from the assistant teacher, who was ready, willing, and able to give and receive hugs from the little citizens of this particular community. Even so, the children wanted so desperately to give the leader of this community a hug throughout the course of the day, but this teacher had an instant reflex that caused her to position her body in such as way that she barred the affection being given to her by the children. If they caught her off guard, they would ambush her legs for a quick second to give her a hug anyway. However, the teacher was still reluctant to embrace the warmth and love the little citizens oh so desperately wanted to express to her.*

*This educator was an excellent instructor academically, but she lacked the ability to reciprocate the love and compassion of the little citizens who sought her approval and love. As a result, the "emotional well" (lead teacher), from which the members of this community should have been able to draw for emotional support, was depleted. This teacher allowed her past hurts and disappointments to dictate her relationship with her little citizens. Seemingly, she was unable to look beyond self in order to be the reliable thermostat the little citizens needed in order to flourish in their community.*

*It was not all hopeless in this community, however; the little citizens were fortunate enough to have an assistant teacher who was just the opposite of the lead teacher. The assistant teacher was not only loving and caring, but she was also steadily tuned in to the children's emotional needs. In short, this assistant teacher was a hugger. The children automatically gravitated more towards her than the lead teacher.*

*This did not settle well with the lead teacher and, over time, she began to despise her fellow coworker. It was apparent in the way she excessively criticized her assistant's performance while interacting with the children. What the lead teacher failed to realize is that she was not only jealous of her assistant teacher, but she was also exposing her own fears, rejections, insecurities, and shortcomings that most likely derived from her past.*

**Note:** I admonish all leaders (i.e., parents, educators, directors, etc.) to be honest with yourself in regards to the limits you may have set for yourself when it comes to giving of self to others. Ask yourself this question: "Are there limitations in my life that will infringe on my ability to develop and maintain an emotionally supportive community?" Bring to the surface your hurts, fears, insecurities, and/or inadequacies so that you can properly address them and move on and focus more on being the best leader you can be. Children do not understand why you cannot give them a hug or smile; all they know and expect from you is that you respond in a manner that makes them feel safe and special. Children are unaware of what you experienced in the past, nor do they care, but they can definitely discern what you are projecting at that moment toward them. Finally, children should never be made to feel guilty or to blame for your emotional deficiencies.

---

*There is an emotional, social, and mental kinship that exists between the leader and her little citizens as they grow and develop as a culture.*

---

### What Is an Effective Leader?

So, what is an effective leader? He or she is an individual with a unique, innate ability to look beyond self in order to clearly see the needs of those under her leadership. In essence, when you see the leader, you see the community, and when you see the community, you see the leader. Why? There is an emotional, social, and mental kinship that exists between the leader and her little citizens as they grow and develop as a culture.

An effective leader is known for her unique ability to steer a group of people (little citizens) in the direction that is most profitable for everyone, physically, emotionally, socially, and mentally. I like to say that an effective leader knows when it is appropriate to take a vertical position/role when leading, guiding, instructing, correcting, and protecting his or her little citizens, but can easily switch to a horizontal position/role when validating, loving, nurturing, and supporting the members of the community.

Can we have a reality check here? There will be times when you will not feel like leading anyone, especially children. Being a leader can sometimes—or a lot of times—be physically and mentally draining because you are constantly giving of yourself, constantly depositing into the lives of others. You may be in need of a well-deserved break. Oftentimes, the insurmountable responsibility of being a leader can cause you to feel as though you are just about on empty, with barely enough of you to pour into the lives of those you lead. While you are continually making future plans for the betterment of your citizens, you may neglect moments for yourself, much-needed moments to celebrate you and to reflect on your personal goals and dreams for the future.

Being a leader is a rewarding and fulfilling job, but when your little citizens have gone their separate ways at the end of the day, you need to get back in touch with self by pampering self, resting self, exercising self, enjoying self, and loving self. Whatever part of the self that is in need of love and attention, attend to it accordingly; then, when you return back to your little ones, you can look beyond yourself in order to see the needs of others.

## The Purpose of a Leader

I have found it to be true, over an over again, that when an individual clearly understands the purpose of a thing, he or she not only appreciates its existence, but he also knows how to utilize the thing in order to get the most out of its existence. Let me insert the word *leader or leadership* in place of the word *it* above: when an individual clearly understands the purpose of being a leader, he not only appreciates the purpose of leadership, but he also knows how to utilize leadership in order to get the most out of its existence.

Sadly, there are many educators and/or parents who are aimlessly leading, with no clue of the true purpose for being a leader. So if I can be of any assistance, here are a list of reasons to explain the purpose of a leader:

1. A leader oversees the welfare of those under his leadership. You

have heard the saying or statement, "He has your best interest at heart." What this statement is saying is, for every issue, decision, and/or need that pertains to the community as a whole, you as the leader must take into consideration what must be done so that the members of the community will benefit socially, emotionally, physically, academically, and mentally. Being the overseer of your community is not just about making plans for today, but rather making plans for today that will have a positive impact on tomorrow.

2.  The second purpose for being a leader is not only to recognize, but also to cultivate the gifts and talents on the inside of the little citizens who are under your leadership. A good leader is always monitoring what is going on in his community. It is as if he is stepping back and observing her little citizens in action, analyzing what they can or cannot do, or what seems to come easily for some, but may be difficult for others. The leader is always creating or using familiar activities or assignments that allow the leader to identify the gifts and talents that each little citizen possesses. Then the leader cultivates the little citizen's gifts and/or talents by giving him or her the opportunity to practice using her gifts or talents during the daily operation of the community. For instance, Anna is very talkative. Her conversations are colorful and full of substance for her age. An observant leader would view Anna's advanced communication skills as being a gift that needs to be cultivated, rather than a disruption to the class. As a result, this leader provides doors of opportunity for Anna to operate in the vein she has been gifted in. Having Anna announce the weather forecast in front of her peers before story time would be a perfect opportunity for Anna to put to use her advanced communication skills. You may be thinking, *"What does this have to do with emotional development?"* When a child's emotional needs are properly attended to and not seen as the child misbehaving or being needy, the child can fully concentrate on the agenda of the community. In addition, she can put to use what she has been

gifted to do in a constructive manner. An emotionally supportive community creates a positive atmosphere, which makes the community so fertile that the gifts and talents inside of the citizens can grow, develop, and eventually be explored while they are still in an emotionally safe environment.

3. A leader inspires those whom he leads to honor the vision and to work towards making the vision become a reality. A community without a vision will scatter. Let's be truthful, in a community there are a plethora of mindsets, behaviors, agendas, attitudes, and even emotional needs. But, as we all know, in order for a vision to become a reality, there has to be unity in the thoughts, behaviors, agendas, attitudes, and/or emotions of the citizens and the leader. The purpose of a leader is to constantly encourage, instruct, direct, and even set limitations on what is acceptable and unacceptable when in a pursuit of a vision. A leader who consistently keeps the vision in front of the little citizens, through words and images (i.e., pictures hanging on the wall, etc.), will eventually paint a picture on the canvas of their imaginations that will serve as a reminder of and blueprint for how they should conduct themselves in the community in order for the vision to come to fruition. When the leader genuinely makes the children feel like they are contributing to the vision of the community, emotional distress is minimal.

Leaders, I want you to be aware that keeping children focused on the vision of the community is not as easy as it seems, especially when children have a concern and/or agenda they feel is more important than the vision at hand. So what do you do? Simply maintain a calm composure, readjust your agenda, and focus on what the child (or children) is trying to communicate to you.

Here are a couple of examples of readjusting your plan:

**Example 1.** Samuel came into the community quite proud of what he had in his possession. He had a bright red race car that was purchased by his father, whom he only sees once a week. Suppose you were trying to read a story to the class, and right in the middle of the group discussion regarding the book, Samuel jumped up and rushed over to his cubby to retrieve his bright red race car; he began to show his peers what his father had bought him during his last visit. Now, it is quite obvious that Samuel has put a dent in your lesson plan, or so you think. However, what Samuel was trying to communicate to you is that his emotions are currently attached to this car because it represents his father's love for him; therefore, it is a must that he shares this important moment in his life. Being the people-centered leader you are, you will effortlessly close your book and ask Samuel to come in front of the members of the community and talk about his new car. Now, can you take it a little further by throwing in some concept development? Might you challenge the children to give their opinion and use the canvas of their imaginations by asking the children about the purpose of having a car?

*Whatever part of the self that is in need of love and attention, attend to it accordingly; then, when you return back to your little ones, you can look beyond yourself in order to see the needs of others.*

As a result of being sensitive and flexible, you accomplish the following:

- You validate Samuel by allowing him to share his story about his car.
- You encourage camaraderie amongst his peers by allowing them to celebrate his feelings of happiness regarding the gift he received from his father.
- You recognize that Samuel has an agenda that was the opposite of your vision for the community.

Putting him on display not only redirected his mindset and behavior back towards the vision of the community, but it also took care of his emotional needs. It was a win-win situation all the way around. The journey towards fulfilling the vision still remained intact. Mission accomplished!

**Example 2.** Blake is emotionally attached to time and honesty. These unusual emotional attachments are his reaction to his mother, who consistently lied to Blake regarding the time she would return home to tuck him into bed. You see, Blake's mother has a strong, addictive relationship with drugs that prohibited her from keeping her word with her son. As a result, Blake would stay awake in the late hours of the night, anxiously waiting for his mom to come home. His mother's addictive behavior not only contributed to Blake being overly consumed with time, but it also caused him to distrust adult figures.

---

*Being the overseer of your community is not just about making plans for today, but rather making plans for today that will have a positive impact on tomorrow.*

---

What do you do? Blake needs consistency in his life. It is quite evident that his home "community" is unable to provide him with what he needs in order to be emotionally and mentally settled. If his home is not providing him with what he needs (respect, security, and honesty), then it is left up to you to make sure that his school community is more efficient in time management and honoring commitments. It could be as simple as you letting Blake know ahead of time that there has been a change in the schedule as it relates to a particular assignment and/or modification of a daily routine. Knowing to expect a change in timing will prevent Blake from becoming emotionally distressed. Also, you could give Blake a job as a time monitor, which allows him to keep track of the time (i.e., setting the timer, etc.) that has been allocated for daily events in his school community. Being consistent and honest will definitely cause Blake to gravitate towards you and embrace his community for the emotional support he is unfortunately deprived of at home. His mother may mean well, but she is having an affair with drugs, which is consuming her mind, emotions, and health.

# Self-Centered vs. People-Centered Leader

Throughout this chapter, I have briefly touched on the differences between being a self-centered leader versus a people-centered leader. Let's review the definition of each type of leader and then briefly look at the characteristics of each.

A **self-centered leader** is an individual who is consumed with self to the point that he or she is constantly searching for things or people to keep him or her comfortable. As a result, she neglects those around her. In other words, this type of leader is selfish.

A **people-centered leader** is a person who is balanced. She understands self, knows how to share self, and knows how to look beyond self for the betterment of others. A people-centered leader is sensitive to the needs of others and can lead them in such a way that the citizen or citizens she oversees can go from one level of maturity to the next.

## Characteristics of a Self-Centered Leader:

- Occupied with self, emotionally, mentally, physically, socially, etc.
- Insensitive to the needs of others
- Only concerned with her progress in life
- Emotionally insensitive to others
- Would rather be heard than listen
- Willing to sacrifice the well-being of the citizens for the sake of forcing her own vision to become a reality

## Characteristics of a People-Centered Leader:

- Constantly surveying the community to see what is required to help the citizens grow and develop into productive little citizens
- Takes pleasure in the progress and accomplishments of the little citizens she oversees

- Sensitive to the emotional, mental, physical, social, and academic needs of the members of the community
- Would rather listen than to be constantly heard
- Flexible and recognizes when change is required for the betterment of the community as a whole
- Cognitive of the goals that must be obtained for the fulfillment of the vision, but at the same time, will not sacrifice the welfare of the little citizens to reach the goal if she feels they are not ready

## The Positive Impact of a People-Centered Leader

To have the strongest possible impact, a people-centered leader must continuously confirm the existence of the community through genuine love and emotional support. This will allow the little citizen not only to feel wanted, but also to feel secure in who he currently is and what he has the potential to become. A people-centered leader is always looking beyond self in order to see the needs of others. *You* are a people-centered leader. Let this be your daily declaration.

Let's be real. You are the next best thing to their parents (and/or caregiver). For those whose biological parents are negligent in fulfilling their parental obligations, you are mentally, physically, and emotionally standing in proxy, either as a mother or father figure. These little citizens are taking a chance by trusting you to take care of them during the day, in the absence of their parents. They trust and depend on you to direct them where they need to go during their developmental milestones. Your little citizens are basking in your presence and depending on you to be sensitive to their emotional needs so that they can focus on being productive in life. They are comfortable in showing you their not-so-good side, knowing you will assist them in making the appropriate adjustments to get back in the flow with the community. They have fallen in love with you and have great admiration for you because you are a people-centered leader who cares.

# Reflections

# Reflections

# Reflections

*One's identity serves as a physical representation of self that is perpetually reaffirmed through one's thoughts, displayed through one's actions, and supported or embraced by one's emotions.*

# Chapter 4

## The Community's Identity

The third key to developing an emotionally supported community is to establish an identity for your community. *Identity*, according to *Merriam Webster*, is the qualities, beliefs, etc., that make a particular person or group different from others. One's identity serves as a physical representation of self that is perpetually reaffirmed through one's thoughts, displayed through one's actions, and supported or embraced by one's emotions. The ultimate purpose of having an identity is that it allows an individual the ability to draw from who he or she is in an effort not only to relate and understand self, but also to relate and understand others. Just as humans are in need of an identity to substantiate their existence, your community is in need of what I call a "universal identity" to authenticate its existence. A community is definitely not a living being, but it does come to life when populated by people.

The purpose of establishing a universal identity for your community is to bring oneness—mentally, socially, and emotionally—among the citizens of the community. The universal identity you select for your community will, over the course of time, take root in the mindset of your little citizens, causing them to bring to life their community identity through their behavior. Oneness is significant from the standpoint that it increases the productivity level within the community; it assists in making the vision of the community a reality; it sets the emotional tone for the community; and it allows the little citizens to get the most out of what the community has to offer.

*I was conducting emotional support training in Eatonton, Georgia. There was a young man by the name of Marcus who was known for his excellent people-centered skills. As I was conversing with his director and the educational coordinator during the lunch break, they could not give Marcus enough praise for his unique ability to connect with the children in his community. As my ears were being flooded with genuine compliments regarding this young man's performance, I could not help but wonder what was the secret behind his success. Marcus indicated that the identity he chose to adopt for his community was the word focus. He paired this particular word with a behavior, a tangible expression. He took his index finger and his middle finger and pointed towards his eyes, then redirected the same two fingers and pointed towards his little citizens to visually connect with them. This was their reminder to stay focused. Eventually, the little citizens began to adopt the identity of the community (focus) as being their very own; as a result, Marcus's community is excelling academically, socially, emotionally, and mentally.*

Let me mention that the longevity of your community's identity is solely dependent on your faithfulness to keeping the universal identity alive through your own actions. You, the people-centered leader, must be the first to believe in the identity that you have selected to define your community, and then let it become part of who you are. This must happen before you can expect your little citizens to do the same. Like leader, like followers!

The second reason for establishing a universal identity for your community is that it sets a standard or a level of expectation—emotionally, socially and mentally—for not only the current little citizens, but also for any newcomers. In essence, the universal identity becomes the trademark for your community, their community.

You are quite aware that children are interested in knowing what you expect of them. Why? They are so excited about life and the discoveries to be made. Their little world is about them, and oftentimes—well, a lot of times—they can be easily distracted. By having an identity already in place, you are at an advantage. While the existing little citizens are becoming more and more like the identity that has been established, the newcomers have the opportunity to see the physical reality of the community through the little citizens' actions and, therefore, can emulate the behavior of their fellow members accordingly.

Marcus was faithful in exemplifying the community's identity, focus, in the presence of his little citizens to the point that they were beginning not only to patrol each other, but they were also showing the new little citizens how to honor the identity of the community.

A third reason for creating a universal identity for your community is to promote emotional wellness for the members as a whole. What I am about say is more so for the school environment, rather than the home environment. Developing emotional wellness for the community at school can be challenging, though not impossible, because each citizen represents a different home environment. The mindset, emotions, and behaviors within these environments can range from functional to dysfunctional and everything in between. As a result, there are a variety of thoughts, emotions, and behaviors that are (or can be) the opposite of what the community's identity represents. And that's ok! Why? Working with little citizens is definitely a learning and growing process for both you and the little citizens. You will find that, over time, if you employ patience, the child will eventually incorporate the universal identity into who he is. Therefore, eventually, the thoughts, emotions, and actions that are attached to the community's identity will replace the thoughts, emotions, and actions that may contradict the identity of the community.

Emotional wellness is not instantaneous, but rather, it is a process. It is during this process that you will discover how children's thoughts, emotions, and physical actions may be in total opposition to the identity that has been customized for the community. Regardless of how the little citizens think or act, they are still members of the community, and the identity of the community does not readjust for the child, but rather the child has to readjust—emotionally, mentally, and behaviorally—in order to come into agreement with the existing identity of the community.

Therefore, by consistently exposing your children to the identity (i.e., having everyone say they are smart throughout the day, etc.), you are constantly reinforcing the identity of the community by creating an image on the canvas of their imagination through words. Words produce thoughts; thoughts trigger emotions; and emotions affect behavior. So if one of your little citizens is having a bad day and biting everyone who crosses his or her path, this does not change his identity. He just needs someone to acknowledge, interpret, and address what he is trying to communicate through his emotions and behavior. I will discuss how to interpret a child's emotions later on. It should be noted here that there are children with severe emotional and behavioral problems that require in-depth therapeutic intervention from a licensed counseling professional. Know your limits, and get the child help as needed.

## The How of Establishing a Community Identity

The right word (or words) makes all the difference when establishing an identity for your community. Words are so powerful that they can determine the course or direction of your community—either positively or negatively. I challenge all the people-centered leaders not to rush, but to take your time in selecting a word or words that will define the identity of the community in a positive and productive way. Eventually, it will become a reality in the lives of your little citizens.

In other words, choosing the right word to define the identity of your community will have a tremendous influence on the citizens' academic performance, in addition to their social, emotional, and mental development. If you are not still convinced, just do an identity test for a couple of months and use the word *failure* to define the identity of your community. Your little citizens' thoughts, emotions, and behavior will eventually become centered on being a failure. A hopeless situation, I would add! A community designed for failure is definitely not a good thing.

Look at how words can dictate what we do or how we feel throughout the day. For example, you tell your friend that you are going to the bank after work. The statement, "I'm going to the bank after work," automatically produces a thought of being at the bank; then it triggers an emotion (either pleasurable or unpleasurable); and finally, it causes an action of getting in the car and going to the bank to take care of your financial matters. The power of words is significant and definitely should not be taken lightly, especially when you have children depending on you to create an environment that will bring maximum results, both academically and developmentally.

Finally, choose a word or words for your little citizens to declare over their lives that will give them strength and a sense of purpose. Let's briefly look at the benefits of choosing the right identity through the right words:

- It will produce emotional resilience amongst the citizens of the community. This means that by presenting the right identity through carefully chosen words, you help stabilize the children's emotions. When they do experience challenges in life, they can spring back and continue on with their day. Granted, no one is exempt from experiencing negative emotions, but students do not have to follow the negative direction emotions want to lead them.

- It creates a mental blueprint through words, a map that will guide the children in the way in which they should go in order to become what they were destined to be.

- Choosing the right identity through words creates an image (i.e., being brave, confident, smart, etc.) on the inside of a child that, once believed and acted upon, will become a physical reality in their lives.

- An identity established by right words will give the little citizens a strong sense of self-worth and belonging.

## Reinforcing the Identity

By exposing the children's eye gate and ear gate to the universal identity of the community through various implementations of songs and activities, you are constantly keeping the identity on the forefront of their minds, which, in return, confirms who they are and reminds them of how they should behave.

Sadly, there are some communities who are experiencing what I call "emotional traffic jams," simply because they have not taken the time to assign a universal identity to represent their community. What they fail to realize is that assigning an identity to their community can assist in redirecting the emotional traffic so that so the atmosphere within the community remains clear and positive. A clear and positive atmosphere allows the little citizens the opportunity to fully concentrate on learning, becoming, sharing, developing relationships, and enjoying life in general.

I would recommend the following activities to be used to reinforce the identity of the community.

**The Identity Shout Out:** This attention-getter activity can be used all through the day. You simply shout out the word you selected for the community's identity and have the children repeat after you. For instance, you would say, "Everyone stay strong." Then the little citizens repeat after you. This is an effective way to bring the members of the community together when you are trying to their get attention to listen, to following instructions, or to shift from one activity to another. You can also just shout it out as a form of declaration. The identity of the community should be voiced throughout the day so that it becomes a reality to all those who hear it. Reinforcing, constantly saying the word that associated with the identity, becomes a powerful tool, which brings to pass the physical reality of the identity at hand.

**Songs, Songs, and More Songs:** Music is a universal language that everyone can relate to. Finding songs that reinforce the identity of the community keeps a melody in the children's heart and mind as it reminds them who they are and what they are capable of becoming. A music playlist with songs that are centered around the identity of your community can be used during certain times of the day in order to maintain the presence of the identity before the citizens of the community. Remember, repetition is very important for children, for it signifies stability.

Here are some music CD's from the renowned children's musical artist Shawn Brown. He has a plethora of songs that will help you to reinforce the identity of your community. Check out *Born to Win*, a socio-emotional development CD, and *I Celebrate You*. You can go on his website, superfunshow.com, to purchase these "identity reinforcement products."

Finally, here are list of positive words and phrases you can use for creating the identity of your community:

| | | |
|---|---|---|
| 1. Born to win | 11. Wisdom | 21. Focused |
| 2. Strong | 12. Talented | 22. I am important |
| 3. Confident | 13. Gifted | 23. Big heart |
| 4. Smart | 14. Harmony | 24. Kindhearted |
| 5. Intelligent | 15. Achievers | 25. Productive |
| 6. Love | 16. I am brave | 26. Teamwork |
| 7. Unity | 17. Champions | 27. Big dreamer |
| 8. Joyful | 18. Peaceful | 28. Caring |
| 9. Happy | 19. Success | 29. Respectful |
| 10. Purpose | 20. Good listeners | 30. I am valuable |

# Reflections

# Reflections

*The mental movies that are playing in the minds of your little citizens have a point of origin that helps explain why children think the way they think, say the things that they say, and do the things that they do.*

# The Mental Movie of Your Community

Every child who attends your community (school environment) or actually lives in your community (home environment) has a movie or movies that play in his or her mind. Now, I am not referring to the movies that the child watches on television, nor am I referring to a particular movie that a child has seen at the theater; rather, I am alluding to the movie that is created in the child's mind by the most famous actors and actresses in his life: parents, caregivers, aunts, uncles, siblings, neighbors, and/or teachers. The negative and positive words, emotions, and behaviors, which are constantly being expressed day in and day out by these highly admired celebrities, becomes the script the child uses to engage in life. And as we all well know, there are a lot of different scripts that are dictating the thoughts of your little citizens. Sadly, some scripts may need a few changes—or even a total revision—before the mental movie can actually be presented, physically, to others. The initial script that makes up the mental movie within a child's mind is centered around the following: the perception of self; the perception of others; the perception of how to interact with others; and the perception of how to respond to life's events and situations. That is why it is important for the initial script presented by his parents be solid enough to assist the little citizen in getting the most out of his exploration of his surroundings, with a limited amount of negative distractions.

## The Origin of Mental Movies

The mental movies that play in the minds of your little citizens have a point of origin that helps explain why children think the way they think, say the things they say, and do the things they do. The point of origin of children's mental movies rightfully begins within what I call the "primary community" (better known as the home environment). Various family interactions, including beliefs, values, and morals, are introduced to the children from birth on. These various family interactions are the generational composition of the family structure. For example, how the family resolves problems, communicates with one another, and shows respect to each other will mark the child. The emotional disposition of the family as a whole, the affection level of family members, and the family's views of others outside of the family system will also mold the way the child thinks. The generational composition of a family structure establishes what I call "prepackaged patterns"—mental, emotional, social, moral and behavioral patterns—that dictate how a child will respond, talk, and act when faced with pleasant and not so pleasant events in life. Prepackaged patterns are acquired skills a child uses to navigate the world through interaction with others in his environment.

Prepackaged patterns give the observer (i.e., teacher, etc.) a general idea of what is taking place in a child's home environment. This can be beneficial in that it not only allows the teacher the opportunity to employ sensitivity, but it also helps her plan how she is going to effectively address the behavior that requires redirecting.

For example, Samanda is very sarcastic and disrespectful towards her teacher and peers—to the point that no one wants to be around her. A mandatory meeting was scheduled to meet Samanda's parents to discuss her behavior at school. The teacher, Mrs. Smith, and the school director, Mrs. Whales, have had the privilege to meet Samanda's mother, but this would be the first time for the both of them to have the opportunity to meet her father. Samanda's mother was very nice and soft spoken, but the father was totally the opposite. He was very cold, sarcastic, and disrespectful to both the teacher and the director. The fruit does not fall far from the tree! Samanda was mentally exposed to her father's negative emotions, words, and behavior to the point that it not only took root in her thoughts, but it also became a reality through her actions.

> *Prepackaged patterns are acquired skills a child uses to navigate the world through interaction with others in his environment.*

In essence, it is the child's mindset that will determine the emotional stability and appropriateness of his behavior, both in public and private. In many cases, a child is labeled as being "bad" or a "problem child," without even taking into consideration that there is a movie playing in the child's mind as a result of her home community. In other words, a child can only do what has been modeled before her.

I recall a little boy who witnessed his father physically abuse his mother from the time he was an infant to age five. His parents eventually got a divorce, but the mental movie of anger, violence, and disrespect still lingered behind. As a result, this little boy's prepackaged patterns were being displayed both at home and school. The teacher automatically labeled him as being a problem child, without first considering the type of mental movie that was playing in his mind. It was quite obvious that this little citizen needed some of the scenes in his mental movie to be tweaked or totally rewritten in order for him to function properly both at home and school.

## It Starts in the Mind

The mind! The mind! The mind! It all starts in the mind. What you are going to have for breakfast in the morning starts in your mind. What you plan to wear to work starts in your mind. The reality of our world begins in our mind. Our thoughts are lived out through our physical actions, as well as the words we speak, and all is based on what we believe. This also holds true for the little citizens in our community. Children's perception of life is an extension of their parents' approach to life—be it functional or dysfunctional. What the little citizens have been conditioned to believe will determine the way in which they socially and emotionally respond to life situations and/or events.

Every child's reality is not only different, but also sacred. Think about it. If every child in your community had an opportunity to dominate the community through his or her preconceived notion of life, there would be disharmony in the community. In addition, the emotional and even the social baseline that was initially established for the community would eventually become insignificant to its members. Now, I am not saying to totally disregard the little citizen's perception of life that he or she has grown accustomed to, but rather to help those who may require more assistance in redirecting their thoughts, especially those thoughts which lead the child to display physical actions that can weaken the emotional and social wellness of the community. That is to say, a child's negative behavior that is a byproduct of his thoughts and emotions should never reach the level that it begins to compete with prescribed thoughts, emotions, and behaviors of the community.

Assisting a child in readjusting his or her thoughts does not happen automatically, but rather it is a process that requires time and patience. The readjustment process consists of the following steps:

1. Target the negative behavior that requires a course of action. If a child has multiple behaviors that need to be addressed, focus on one behavior at a time. It can be overwhelming

for a child to readjust his or her thoughts for every negative behavior he displays, especially a young child (i.e., pre-schooler) whose thought process is so impressionable.

2. Constantly expose the child's mind to the desired behavior, either through modeling, educational resources, or subtle redirection of the child's attention towards one of his peers who is modeling the desired behavior (i.e., "I like how Johnny is sharing the fire truck with Adam.").

3. Display an emotions chart on the wall with various emotions illustrated. This will allow the child to identify where he is currently and where he desires to be.

4. Once the child has selected the desired emotion, then assist the child in developing a "workable" plan to obtain the desirable behavior.

5. Help the little citizen create his own simple, positive statement that he can say throughout the day. This simple, positive statement has a two-fold purpose:

   a) It enables the child to constantly confirm what he is capable of being and doing by undertaking this change.
   b) Simple, positive statements create new mental images of the desired physical action in the child's mind and replace the old mental image that is attached to the undesirable behavior.

6. Provide praise to the child when you observe him displaying the desired behavior. Also, encourage him ("You can do it!")—even when he is regressing back to his old actions.

## The Mental Movie of Your Community

What mental movie is playing in your community? What is the theme of your mental movie? What type of emotional and social script did you use to develop the mental movie of the community? What are the underlying themes presented in this mental movie? Does the mental movie of the community have what it takes, not only to meet the social, emotional, mental, and physical needs of the little citizens, but also to equip them to advance in life? Bottom-line: the mental movie of the community should be influential enough to persuade its little citizens to change the channel in their minds, enabling them to effectively flow with the rules, routines, and overall agenda of the community.

*A child's negative behavior that is a byproduct of his thoughts and emotions should never reach the level that it begins to compete with prescribed thoughts, emotions, and behaviors of the community.*

All of these questions are pertinent from the standpoint that the mental movie of the community must be reliable enough, strong enough, and influential enough to steer the little citizens in the direction that leads to mental, social, emotional, and physical wellness. Could you even imagine being in a community surrounded by a bunch of little citizens whose minds are on every other channel but the main channel that plays the mental movie of the community? This is comparable to being in a room filled with flat screen televisions, turned on different channels, playing simultaneously. Too much! Right? At least you have the option to turn all the flat screens off or select the one that you want to leave on. Well, when it comes to children, it is a different story altogether; you cannot just switch off the mental movies playing in their minds. However, you definitely can set an atmosphere in the community where the little citizens are being stretched to turn the channel or change the mental movie playing in their minds in order to get in sync with the mental movie of the community.

Getting all of your little citizens on the same channel requires time, patience, and sensitivity. Why? For each mental movie playing in the mind of a child, there are emotional attachments. These emotional attachments are compilations of memories that makeup the mental movies that are playing. If you totally replace the child's mental movie with that of the community—without taking the time to gain some understanding of the emotional ties associated with his or her mental movie—it can possibly cause the child to become physically aggressive towards his or her peers and/or socially withdrawn, thereby interfering with the overall development of the child. Children personalize these mental movies (either good or bad, functional or dysfunctional) to the point that they can become like security blankets, bringing comfort, especially when they are away from their home community.

So how do you effectively promote or advertise the mental movie of the community so that it is watched more frequently in the minds of the citizens than their own mental movies? And how do you encourage the little citizens to make the script of the community's mental movie come alive through their actions?

1. Make sure the mental movie of the community is playing on a regular basis so that the little citizen's mindset is always being exposed to the social and emotional etiquettes of the community. The mental movie of the community should not be playing all day on one day but on pause the next day. Rather, the different scenes contained in the mental movie of the community, such as respect, positive peer relations, positive affection, and adhering to rules, must be modeled through your actions and expressed by the words that come out of your mouth. Thus, the little citizens will incrementally gain a clearer understanding of what is expected of them.

2. Create activities or utilize resources that reinforce the mental movie you prefer the children to watch. This allows the little citizens the opportunity to learn how to conduct themselves accordingly within the confinement of the community. For instance,

present a book to the citizens regarding respect and have an open discussion about respect and the impact it has on self and others.

3. Encourage and recognize when the little citizens are acting out one of the scenes of the community's mental movie. Encouragement and recognition serve as positive incentives that drive the child into wanting to display the behavior more often in effort to receive praise for his or her positive behavior. Being validated by his or her community leader is very important to a child.

4. Subtly direct the child to observe and learn from peers who have easily grasped the social, emotional, mental, and behavioral messages that make the community's mental movie. Encourage the child to implement what he sees.

5. Children are very visual; therefore, create a mental blueprint in each child's mind through relevant posters displayed throughout the community. These visual cues will motive the children to function properly within the confinement of the community. The following four posters (or find a picture and enlarge it to poster size) are a must-have when advertising the mental movie of the community:

   a) A poster of a clean community: little citizens should always participate in the upkeep of the community in order to maintain a nice, consistent flow and to ensure an awareness of where things (i.e., toys, clothing, books, etc.) are when needed.

   b) A poster of children engaging in positive interaction: it is vital that this form of social advertisement remains in the forefront of the little citizens' minds so that they know how to conduct themselves accordingly.

c) A poster of children sitting and attentively listening to the leader (i.e., teacher, parent, etc.) of the community: this form of advertising conveys messages pertaining to respect, focus, and discipline.

d) A poster that presents to your little citizen the possibilities life holds, for example, a picture of a university or a depiction of career options (i.e., fireman, nurse, etc.): this form of advertisement helps the little citizens imagine themselves in the future.

# Reflections

# Reflections

*A purpose station is a place of refuge where a little citizen can constructively vent when he or she is emotionally distressed.*

## The Purpose Station

What do you do when one of the little citizens in your community has an emotional meltdown? Do you just let the citizen fend for himself? Do you leave him, to the best of his ability, to make sense of the emotion or emotions that currently have his undivided attention? Or, do you let the little citizen openly vent his emotions, unsupervised, in the presence of his peers, possibly causing physical harm to others? This last option can also set a harmful precedent as to how to express one's behavior during an emotional crisis.

As I indicated in chapter 1, emotions and/or feelings are real, but one's emotions should never rule over the individual. Being governed by strong emotions can tempt a child to display negative/inappropriate behaviors. I will elaborate more on this scenario later and highlight the importance of teaching our children how to live by principles, not by emotions.

Our emotions and feelings are the unstable part of our psychological makeup. An individual's thoughts are constantly changing from one moment to the next, from one topic to another, both relevant or irrelevant, real and not so real. I don't know about you, but this ongoing "mental aerobics" can be a little bit too much for me at times, so I can only imagine the mental workout a child has when his or her emotions are being tested as he engages with the world.

It is of the utmost importance that you, a people-centered leader, stay open to the fact that your little citizen's emotions are valid and need to be heard. By strategically developing a plan that effectively addresses the emotional needs of those who are under your watch, you will benefit both yourself and the entire community. Being prepared for the emotionally charged moments can mean everything, no matter how big or small your community may be.

So what precautionary measures can you as a community leader take when one of your little citizens is experiencing an emotional crisis? I would like to introduce to you the purpose station. The purpose station is a designated area within your community that becomes a place of refuge where a little citizen (or citizens) can go and seek alternative behavioral patterns. It is designed to assist him to constructively vent when being emotionally challenged.

I have had the opportunity to introduce this concept throughout the United States. I take such pleasure in witnessing how the wheels begin to turn in the minds of educators and parents alike as they begin to visualize a special place in their community that is not only safe, but also a place where a child can properly address those uncomfortable emotions and feelings that oftentimes trigger inappropriate behavioral patterns.

Can you imagine a safe place that is fully equipped to address the specific emotional needs of the children in your community? This place of refuge is well-thought-out. So much so, in fact, that all of those who take advantage of the purpose station can seamlessly transition right back into the rhythm of things, rather than staying disconnected from the community for a long length of time.

## Why Implement a Purpose Station?

A purpose station physically engages the child through solution-based techniques that address the emotional needs of the child in an effort to bring relief. For example, Sara has separation anxiety when her mom drops her off at the daycare provider. Sara becomes so emotionally distressed at the thought of her mother leaving her presence that she begins to wail endlessly, isolating herself from the rest of the members of the community.

Miss Laurie decided that it was high time to create a purpose station capable of properly responding to Sara's distressful moments when separated from her mother. Miss Laurie designated a certain section of the purpose station that she called the arts and crafts section, where little citizens can constructively express their disappointments, hurts, and anxieties in an artistic manner. This particular area of the purpose station was filled with a colorful array of construction papers, markers, and crayons to assist Sara in creating a beautiful card. Now, Sara can present an "I miss you" card to her mother upon her arrival to pick her up.

This simple, but powerful, solution-based technique provides an emotional way of escape for Sara, not only to modify her behavior, but also to redirect her mindset from excessive emotional distress and anxiety to creativity. During this time of regrouping her thoughts and emotions, Sara is being challenged to cognitively embrace other constructive strategies to express how she longs for her mother. In time, her emotions will come into agreement with the new thoughts associated with how to respond in a positive manner when separated from her mother.

## Solution-Based Activities

Solution-based activities are the core of the purpose station. It is careful selection of materials (i.e., colorful construction paper, markers, play-doh, music, etc.) used during the activity (or activities) that will foster emotional, social, and mental wellness for the child who is consumed mentally and emotionally as a result of a stressful event and/or situation. Note: A child is reluctant to move any further (i.e., engage in academic performance) until his or her emotional needs are met.

The solution-based activities you choose to implement within your purpose station, either it be self-created or preexisting must meet the following criteria in order to be considered effective:

1. Provide activities that will help the child get unstuck from his negative emotions.

2. Usher in new emotions that will allow the child to rejoin the community and enjoy a productive day.

3. Offer activities that are appealing, that will tempt the child to try a more appropriate behavior.

Let's consider these criteria. First, the solution-based activity must provide suggestions that challenge the child to replace old thoughts with new thoughts. He must recognize different ways to conduct himself in the event of a emotional meltdown. Going back to the example I used earlier, there was a special section of Miss Laurie's purpose station filled with a variety of hands-on materials, readily accessible for Sara to make her mom an "I miss you" card.

As Sara physically engages in this solution-based activity, her mind is being introduced to new information on how to productively work through the anxiety of being separated from her mother. Over the course of time, old thoughts will eventually be discarded, and new thoughts will be adopted and acted upon accordingly.

The second criteria for a successful purpose station considers the type of activities offered. Solution-based activities must be capable of ushering in those emotions the child can utilize in order to get the most out of his day physically, mentally, socially, emotionally, and academically.

*My husband and I were invited to present at a professional development training event held in Lake City, Florida. The subject matter I presented to the participants of this training was, "How to Develop an Emotionally Supportive Community." In the midst of my presentation, I began to introduce the purpose station, just like I'm presenting to you in this book. During the break, a participant approached me and asked how the purpose station could be effective in redirecting a child who has severe anger outbursts, which are displayed by destroying the classroom (i.e., throwing chairs, etc.) and/or being physically aggressive towards his peers. She went on to say that this little boy is the byproduct of domestic violence and inconsistent parental support. His disengaged mother is in and out of this little boy's life due to her drug-addicted lifestyle. He was receiving counseling, but the educator wanted to know what she could do to help her little citizen properly de-escalate his anger, while at the same time protecting the other members of the community from being physically harmed.*

*I briefly explained to the sincerely concerned educator that her little citizen never had the opportunity to experience a peaceful and nurturing home environment that generated the love and protection he needed to feel safe and wanted by his parents. Consequently, there were scenes of domestic violence and abandonment stuck on repeat mode and constantly replaying in his mind, causing negative emotions to be activated and displayed through his physical actions. In short, this child was angry because of the bad hand he was dealt at an early age.*

*I recommended that she create a purpose station furnished with two bean bags (or something comfortable to lounge on), one for the teacher and the other for the little citizen. Also needed for this solution-based activity is two sets of headphones, a CD player, and a musical playlist that consists of songs gentle to the little listener's ears, such as jazz, nursery rhymes, or socio-emotional development music. The goal of this activity is to usher in the emotion that this little citizen was deprived of experiencing as a result of his unstable home environment.* **Note:** The leader needs to participate in this activity a couple of times (however many times needed) with the little citizen for three reasons:

1. To model the appropriate behavior while executing this solution-based activity.

2. To bring comfort and support to the little citizen as he explores different options to address his emotional meltdown, which, in this case, resulted in physical aggression.

3. To simply let him know that someone cares for his safety and well-being.

This solution-based activity would also provide a serene and safe atmosphere, releasing the love needed to calm and redirect his mindset and trigger emotions more conducive for his community at school. In essence, I was challenging this particular people-centered leader to establish an environment that is totally the opposite from his home environment, in hopes of him adopting the behavioral patterns that would assist him in excelling socially, emotionally, mentally, and academically.

**Note:** The solution-based activities offered at your purpose station are not for a selected few. Rather, the purpose station is open for all little citizens who may or may not be experiencing a challenge. That is, if other members of the community see their peer or peers receiving special attention, they will want to receive the same. There was a community leader, a preschool teacher, who told the story of how she used lavender oil to calm those little citizens who were experiencing anxiety or anger. She would put a small amount of lavender oil in the palm of the hands of each little citizen. Then she would have them rub their hands together, cup their hands to their nose, and begin breathing, taking in the aroma of the lavender oil. This simple, solution-based activity became a big hit amongst her community, so much so that all the little citizens wanted their share of lavender oil.

Make sure your purpose station is colorful, yet soothing in nature so that it will allow the child to consider modifying his or her behavior in order to usher in those emotions that compliment the existing emotional climate of your community.

The third criterion for solution-based activities within your purpose station is that the offerings must be inviting so that the child will likely want to participate. These activities can modify a child's thought processes and behavior patterns over the course of time, but he must first be interested and willing to try it. Little citizens depend heavily on their senses. It is through their senses that they are able to explore their surroundings and learn accordingly. Every solution-based activity contained in your purpose station must stimulate their senses, which will, in turn, write on the canvas of their imagination a more appropriate way to handle distress. That is to say, their senses help create memories that a child can refer to when tempted to regress back to his old behavior patterns.

## Resource Center

The purpose station can serve as a resource center. The little citizens can, as needed, freely utilize the solution-based activities offered. Because the purpose station is readily accessible for the members of the community, it will encourage them to take the initiative to modify their own actions. This is especially true on those days when they are being challenged or consumed with emotions that are more likely to influence them to behave in a negative and/or inappropriate manner.

In one of my presentations to educators, I introduced a solution-based technique that I call "release." This technique is specifically designed for children who have angry outbursts. The materials recommended for this activity are a hula hoop and a mist spray bottle filled with water. (Water is not a requirement; you and your little citizens could pretend that water is inside the bottle.) On the outside of the bottle, put a happy face sticker.

The materials in this technique have symbolic meanings. The hula hoop epitomizes a contained area where the child can safely process and vent his or her anger without causing physical harm to self or others. The spray bottle with the happy face represents shifting from being emotionally disturbed or distressed to being emotionally and mentally calm. This visualization can birth a positive behavior that is safe and beneficial for the child and all his fellow citizens. **Note:** If water is going to be used during this solution-based activity, you should be the one who lightly sprays the child's face as he changes his facial expression from angry/sad to happy. Children can be very creative in finding other ways to use a spray bottle filled with water—if you know what I mean!

I have some helpful guidelines to introduce and implement this activity. First, the community leader can role-play this activity before the whole community, twice a week, on Monday and Friday. Why at those times? Children come in on Monday with emotional baggage accumulated over the weekend in the home environment. These issues need to be resolved so the little citizen can move on and be productive. On Friday, repeating this activity will leave the child with options on how to properly address his angry outbursts if a situation arises while away from school.

Role-play by pretending you are angry. Show the little citizens how to properly use the solution-based activity. This gives the children an opportunity to observe how to properly contain anger and process it in a suitable manner. I highly recommend that you refer to a situation that occurred in the past, involving a child displaying physical aggression as an outburst of anger. You do not have to announce to the whole community who this child is; deep inside, he or she will know who is being portrayed.

By consistently demonstrating this powerful technique (release) in front of your little citizens, they will become aware of this tool to use when they're emotionally distressed. In addition, you will be promoting how to be responsible for one's actions. So I admonish you to create a purpose station in your community, and the children will come to that place of refuge.

# Reflections

# Reflections

# Reflections

*Community meetings are at their best when conversations are created, ideas are birthed, and unity drives the rhythm of the community, all in an atmosphere of discovery.*

## Community Meetings

Have you ever thought about different ways in which you can influence your little citizens to take ownership of their community? Well, I would like to challenge you to start implementing monthly community meetings with your little citizens. You may be laughing right now, or you may be saying to yourself, "Community meetings? Are you serious?" You can laugh if you want to, but if you dare to integrate this event within the operation of your community, you will proudly discover that your little citizens will not only begin to take ownership of their community, but they will also embrace, protect, and enjoy the place that they now call their own.

### Exploring the Whys of Community Meetings

**Why # 1 Emotional and Social Connection:** Children must feel socially and emotionally connected to their community in order to receive all that the community has to offer. This will be one of most important "whys" I present because a community is only as strong as its members. In essence, the little citizens are the community and bring life to the vision of the community as they both adhere to the rules of the community and participate in establishing rules, boundaries, and goals that keep the vision alive.

There are six necessities every child needs in order to feel socially and emotionally connected to his or her community:

- Every child needs to be loved.
- Every child needs to be highly respected.
- Every child needs to be accepted.
- Every child needs to be valued.
- Every child needs to be remembered.
- Every child needs to be understood.

I will never forget a story that I heard about a little girl who was severely ill; it was not certain if she was going to live. While conversing with her family, she made a profound statement. She said, "I am not afraid of dying, but I am afraid that I will not be remembered." Wow!

Every child wants to be loved, valued, respected, accepted, understood, and re-membered, so hold this truth close to your heart and let it resonant in your mind. Then, you will always be attuned emotionally to the needs of your community.

These six essential necessities will give the child inner security, allowing the child to discover his or her niche and develop strong interpersonal and intrapersonal skills. These skills will enable him to be emotionally, physically, mentally, academically, and morally sound.

**Why # 2 Community Contributions:** Once a child has socially and emo-tionally bonded with her community, she begins to contribute by giving her opinions and/or sharing her thoughts. These contributions are directed towards the betterment of the community. No matter how big or small the contribution may be, it is of great importance to have the opportunity to give of one's self.

A community meeting is a great forum for a child to learn how to shift from being completely self-centered to becoming more people-centered. This mental shift challenges the child to take into consideration the views, ideas, and opinions of others, rather than solely thinking, *I need, I want, and I think.* These self-centered thoughts often bring to surface negative emotions that are the byproduct of a child feeling neglected and/or denied of getting her way.

*Emotional and Social Connection: Children must feel socially and emotionally connected to their community in order to receive all that the community has to offer.*

This open forum (community meeting) challenges the child to give of herself; in addition, it teaches the little citizen how to negotiate through brainstorming. By brainstorming, you give the little citizens the opportunity to come up with many options and then select the best option or options—one that is beneficial to everyone. **Note:** Your job as a people-centered leader is to orchestrate the meetings in such a way that everyone is genuinely heard, acknowledged for her input, and guided in making decisions that are advantageous for the community as a whole.

**Why #3 Community Culture:** Community meetings keep the community culture intact so that the emotional well-being of its citizens can be properly attended to. Your community becomes a culture within itself, which influences the citizens to embrace and adopt the community as their own. In other words, the culture of the community becomes part of each child's identity. Each time the children are given the opportunity to participate in community meetings, they embrace their community by sharing their opinions and thoughts. Making suggestions and/or initiating new ideas for the betterment of the community give the children a sense of ownership. Every time the little citizens become emotionally connected to their community through their thoughts, actions, and conversations, it increases the level of respect they have for each entity (leadership, peers) contained within the community. Keep in mind, a culture is not exclusively defined as a particular race or ethnic group; rather, it is a group of people who have a common interest, which they embrace and show high regard for.

**Why #4 Rules and Boundaries:** Community meetings allow you and the little citizens to openly discuss the effectiveness of preexisting rules, and if need be, to introduce new rules that will create, strengthen, and even realign the boundaries required to maintain order within the community. You will find the daily operations of your community depend on a set of rules and established boundaries. Predetermined rules ensure the following:

1. The authoritative position of the leader will be rightfully respected amongst the citizens in the community. Children who hold high regards for their leader are motivated to conduct themselves accordingly. Respect for authority produces a harmonious atmosphere that generates productivity. A harmonious atmosphere generously provides you with more time to concentrate on the activities and lessons that support the overall well-being of children, rather than constantly being distracted by disruptive behaviors.

2. There will always be an approved course of action the little citizens can choose as they mentally, socially, emotionally, behaviorally, and academically navigate through their community.

3. The vision of the community will be consistently reinforced. Over the course of time, the little citizens will reap benefits from such structure as they recognize their community is right and good. The vision of the community draws its strength from the established rules and boundaries, which are strategically set in place. The assigned vision of the community will be discussed in further details in chapter 8.

**Why #5: Achievements and Planning:** Community meetings can be utilized as a platform to give recognition both individually and collectively to those who either contributed to and/or made sacrifices for the advancement of the community. As I stated earlier in this chapter, contributions are the ideas, opinions, and efforts that are genuinely and generously rambled off by your little citizens. Sacrifice is made by a citizen when one modifies the attitude or behavior that can so easily stagnate the growth of a community if it is allowed to remain as is.

*Community meetings allow you and the little citizens to openly discuss the effectiveness of preexisting rules, and if need be, to introduce new rules that will create, strengthen, and even realign the boundaries required to maintain order within the community.*

When children are recognized for their accomplishments, they are more emotionally and socially fused with the community; mentally in tune with and focused on the task that has been set before them; confident in what they are capable of doing and becoming; and reassured that they are on the right path.

It is important for me to interject that during a community meeting always, always, always make a point to start off with words of encouragement and acknowledgments *before* transitioning to the concerns and deficiencies within the community. For example, your little citizens are endlessly being challenged to share with one another. This deficiency, selfishness, is brought up during a meeting. You, the people centered-centered leader, present to your little citizens a systematic plan that would foster sharing amongst the members of the community, thereby giving everyone an opportunity to play with highly sought after toys and/or to participate in exciting educational projects. You encourage the members of your community to assist in the creating phase of this plan. You give them input by allowing them to determine and assign colors to the toys and projects that are the most popular. So, in essence, you are bringing

THE PRODUCTIVE LITTLE CITIZENS

to the members' attention their weak point; then you present a plan that calls for their participation in order to properly execute the plan. Or, you can start from scratch by assisting the little citizens in brainstorming to come up with their own plan to defeat selfishness and promote sharing. Either method you choose, the children are activating their higher order thinking skills as they work together in creating a plan that will resolve the problem and help the community excel to the next level. Remember, always start off the meeting with achievements, recognition, and words of encouragement before transitioning into the areas of concern.

**Why #6 Growth and Learning:** Community meetings are not always about having an agenda. Granted, having an agenda is important, in that it brings order, but what do you do when the unexpected shows up and challenges the order of things? Suppose one of the little citizens just lost a loved one. What if all of a sudden, her fellow peers quietly get up during the meeting to go over and give her hugs as a form of emotional support during her time of grief? Or, what if a child who normally makes it a point to isolate himself from others met a new friend and wants to openly announce the good news to all those who will listen? Unexpected life events and experiences can cause what I call "memorable shifts" to occur, even in the midst of order. A memorable shift is when something emotionally, socially, or mentally changes within an individual as he learns and grows from the experience at hand. These shifts leave behind memories that can be reflected on when in need of strength, confidence, courage, laughter, or reassurance.

**Why #7 Building and Maintaining Trust:** Trust should always be the central theme of your community. For it is trust that confirms the realization that people need people. People need people for support, understanding, encouragement, relationship, and accountability. By gathering the little citizens together for a community meeting, you give them the chance to get better acquainted with each other while engaging in human relationship. This will open doors of opportunities for them to explore their surroundings, either individually or collectively, in order to receive what is required for them to grow and develop into productive little citizens.

82

Trust is also built and maintained through community meetings when the children physically observe and intentionally sense your commitment to having their best interest at hand. Remember, trust gives the children the freedom to explore and receive what they need in order to be productive little citizens.

I would like to add the final touches to this chapter by giving you a sample agenda of how a community meeting can be conducted with your little citizens. Keep in mind that every community is different, so let this sample agenda serve as a guide and not a law.

## Sample Community Meeting

### I. Ice Breaker
Select a song and/or activity centered on the topic or topics to be discussed during the meeting.

Reason: Purposely choosing songs and/or activities that contain key words will condition the little citizens' minds to be in sync with the topic/issues to be discussed during the meeting.

Length of time: five to seven minutes

### II. Recognition and Words of Encouragement
Reason: It is important for children to be recognized for contributions and/or sacrifices made for the betterment of the community. It confirms that they are doing well and are on the right track. Words of encouragement substantiate a child's existence, thereby making him want to try harder.

Length of time: two to three minutes

### III. Presenting to the Community
Reason: When you present new ideas to the community, it will increase the little citizens' level of awareness regarding the topic at hand. It will stimulate

involvement from the children as they learn more about the operation and maintenance of the community.

Length of time: no time limit. All citizens must have a clear understanding of the topics before proceeding to the open forum.

## IV. Open Forum

Reason: Allowing the little citizens to contribute their opinions and give suggestions will promote participation and ownership.

Benefits of the open forum: (1) autonomy; (2) high regards for a child's views; (3) intellectual conversation; (4) positive peer relationships;(5) higher order thinking skills; (6) language development; (7) brainstorming; and (8) advanced social and emotional skills.

Length of time: open

**Note:** Some topics (issues and/or concerns) may not be resolved in one meeting. As a result, it is best that the topic of concern be "left on the table" and picked up at the next community meeting. Not being in a rush to resolve or address a particular topic teaches the children patience.

## V. Conclusion/Wrap It Up

Reason: This last phase of the community meeting is for summarizing what has taken place during the meeting. Highlight key points and review the plan of action to be taken. This part of the meeting is beneficial to the members because it not only increases their ability to recall information, but it also increases their level of comprehension.

Length of time: five minutes

**Note:** Take a wiggle break with music or some form of movement activity if citizens start to wander off physically or mentally.

# Reflections

_____

_____

_____

_____

_____

_____

_____

_____

_____

_____

# Reflections

# Reflections

## The Community's Assigned Vision

Without a vision, the little citizens can go astray. Your community should always be in a state of progression, not regression. The only way you and your little citizens can successfully be in a state of progression is by personalizing a vision. This vision will establish the course of direction for your community and will eventually bring everyone into harmony mentally, emotionally, socially, and behaviorally. This will help you achieve the tangible manifestation of your vision. I call this type of vision an assigned vision.

A community in forward motion will not become stagnate, nor will it get off track when internal or external influences come on the scene. That is, the members of the community will make the necessary changes in order to stay on course as they pursue the assigned vision of the community.

*During our heavy season of travels, I had the honor to chitchat with one of the educators who expressed how her community was becoming more and more culturally diverse. She did not feel fully prepared for the shifts and changes that were taking place in her community as a result of this external influence (community becoming more diverse). Not only was this external influence bringing about change to the broader community, but it was also bringing internal changes to her classroom (i.e., lack of resources, etc.) that were compounding the problem.*

*She lacked the resources (i.e., easy access to an interpreter, etc.) to effectively communicate and teach her non-English speaking citizens. This external influence bred internal influences (i.e., lack of resources, etc.) so quickly that the educator was not fully equipped to accommodate them. As a result, the little citizens were not getting the most out of what the community had to offer. This caused her non-English speaking citizens to become emotionally distressed, socially deprived, and academically challenged. Keep in mind that the assigned vision is not for a selected few, but for all those who make up the community.*

## What Is an Assigned Vision?

An assigned vision is a customized mental image of one's self (or community) in the future. This customized view of self becomes the blueprint an individual and/or group of people can use to work towards the goal. By keeping his or her assigned vision in the front of their mind, an individual adopts the thoughts, actions, and words—even resources—that are in sync with the process of transforming a mental image into a physical reality.

An assigned vision has no physical presence; that is, it is not apparent to one's physical senses, but the assigned vision does have a mental presence, which is exclusively painted on the canvas of one's imagination until it makes its grand entrance into the life or lives of those who have been diligent and patient in waiting for the manifestation.

The initial stage of an assigned vision usually starts off as a written plan or strategy, keeping the desired end state in mind. This written plan is either posted on a wall, refrigerator and/or bathroom mirror, or on a bulletin board, depending on whether it is a home or school goal. It may even be transcribed in a work manual for employees to observe and acknowledge. The written phase of a vision is what creates a mental picture that gives direction, builds expectation, takes preparation, and requires determination in order to catapult the vision into a state of motion.

> *Your community should always be in a state*
> *of progression, not regression.*

### A Customized Vision at Its Best

*There was a distinguished gentleman directing a Head Start Program in Amarillo, Texas. As he took my husband and me on a tour of his state-of-the-art facility, the director indicated that from day one he declared his program was the number one program in the United States. He diligently made sure this declaration was publicly announced on a daily basis throughout his facility until each and every staff member adopted the thoughts, actions, and words that were in agreement with the customized vision (assigned vision) he had created for the program. His mental goals finally became a physical reality—all because he had a vision.*

To summarize, an assigned vision is a customized mental image that captures one's hopes for self or group in the near future. This personalized mental image of a goal or desirable state becomes a blueprint, defining the specific actions, words, thoughts, and resources necessary to achieve your vision.

At the end of this chapter, I will give simple steps to customize a vision specifically for your community. After all, the success of your community is heavily dependent on the vision you have established for your community. With that in mind, let's look at the purpose and relevance behind formulating an assigned vision for your community.

## The Purpose of an Assigned Vision

In my book, *What All Children Want: Structure*, I indicated that until a person understands the purpose of a thing, he will not consider it important, neither will he understand how to properly make use of it. Let's clarify the purpose of an assigned vision.

**Purpose #1 Assigned Vision Provides Direction.** A vision is unreachable unless you are facing the proper direction: the future. An assigned vision assists you in establishing a plan that will escort your community members from where they currently are to the place where you desire them to be. During the transition of leaving one developmental level (i.e., socially, emotionally, etc.), a plan must be in place to help navigate the little citizens to the desirable state of being. So, in essence, the plan you choose will serve as the compass to point in the direction of your vision. With the path clearly marked, both you and your little citizens can pursue the vision accordingly. Always remember, you and your little citizens were never meant to go where you cannot see.

**Purpose #2 Stay Connected to the Possibilities.** Never foster an environment where your little citizens, or you, the people-centered leader, become complacent with the here and now, but rather always challenge them to stay connected with the possibilities of life by displaying posters on the wall of the community or by leading group discussions, etc. An assigned vision unleashes the possibilities to take the little citizens to the next level, socially, emotionally, mentally, physically, and academically. Staying connected to the possibilities of life keeps you looking at your little citizens from the position of what they are capable of becoming, rather than where they currently are. How many of you can attest to the fact that there are some precious darlings out there who can make it quite difficult to see past their current behavior?

Not only will the little citizens get a glimpse of what they are capable of having or being, but they will also become more mature as they participate in executing the plan for the assigned vision.

**Purpose #3 Flow with the Underlying Current.** Constantly moving with the underlying current of the vision produces an expansion of growth, allowing the leader and her citizens to excel from one level to the next. Why? There is a level of maturity gained, individually and collectively, as the community migrates in the direction of the assigned vision by actively participating in implementing the established plan. Resisting the forward movement of the assigned vision can put the vision in a dormant state, where it will be eventually forgotten.

---

*An assigned vision is a customized mental image of one's self (or community) in the future*

---

**Purpose #4 Keep the Answer before You.** Whenever you are dealing with people, you will have conflicting moments, just because everyone is different. Whenever a group of people congregate, each brings his own will, agenda, and attitude, all of which generates conflict and derails the group from seeing a solution where a problem exists. By having an assigned vision, you are constantly keeping the answer before your little citizens as you and your members address the problems at hand and embark on a better future for all.

**Purpose #5 Stay in Your Lane.** Another purpose of an assigned vision is to disciple you and your little citizens to stay in your own lane. Do not occupy your mind with what another community may have or not have, what they are doing and not doing. What might be conducive for one community may not be conducive for another. It is important, as a leader, to never put yourself in a position where you are always comparing yourself to other leaders and/ or comparing your little citizens with theirs. Rather, stay in the lane that will take you and your little citizens to your vision, the possibilities and the next developmental level that is specifically designed for you and your members. Your vision defines the lane that has been exclusively set for your community. When you stay in your lane, all the resources, discoveries, fulfillment, and maturity (social, emotional, and mental) will come to fruition in your community. I said it once; I said it twice; I will say it once again: stay in your lane.

**Purpose #6 Get out of the Stuck Mode.** A community that is perpetually in a stagnate mode will always be passed by for a promotion. Sadly, there are a lot of communities out there, home and school environments alike, that are experiencing some form of growth delay, academically, socially, emotionally, or even mentally. Creating and diligently implementing an assigned vision eliminates stagnation and begins to stimulate growth. Stagnation is addressed through a vision that is filled with solutions. The key to eliminating apathy within a community setting is having another vision already in place, ready to go, once the current vision is physically tangible and in operation.

## Importance of Possessing an Assigned Vision

Now that I have presented the purpose of having an assigned vision, let's go a step further by examining the whys or the importance of possessing an assigned vision.

The level of importance given to an assigned vision will determine not only the level of success, but also the level of strength (mentally, socially, emotionally, and academically) the members will obtain during their journey to fulfilling the vision.

Even though visions vary from one community to another, there should always be a common core that solidifies the existence or the importance of a vision as it pertains to the growth and development of the little citizens.

**1. Vision Considers What Your Community Needs.** An assigned vision takes into consideration everything your little citizens need in order to experience wholeness, emotionally, socially, mentally, physically, academically, and morally. I refer to these areas as the "wholesome six." The wholesome six must be measurable in a child's life before wholeness can become a reality. For example, a child can be a genius, but at the same time, socially withdrawn. As a result, the opportunity to fully experience wholeness is limited because these essential elements (social development, emotional development, etc.) are not properly balanced so that the child can thrive. Therefore, during the process of establishing an assigned vision, you, the people-centered leader, must capture the big picture of the community, which entails meeting the mental, educational, academic, physical, and moral requirements of the community, so that all your little citizens can experience wholeness.

---

*Staying connected to the possibilities of life keeps you looking at your little citizens from the position of what they are capable of becoming, rather than where they currently are.*

---

**2. Tap into the Preexisting Potential.** The second reason why it is important to have an assigned vision for the community is that it taps into the preexisting potential that dwells within each and every little citizen you oversee. An assigned vision not only allows your little citizens to discover their potential, but it also allows them to contribute their newly discovered potential towards the betterment of the community as a whole.

A vision has the unique ability to provoke the untapped potential that resides on the inside of the little citizen to rise to the surface. The child gains an awareness of what he is capable of doing, having, and being. Another definition of self is being introduced to the little citizens as they physically and mentally participate in the plans specially designed to bring about the tangible reality of the vision.

**3. Conduct Oneself Accordingly.** Any assigned vision, also referred to as a customized vision, worth pursuing will place a demand on the visionaries (you and your citizens) to conduct themselves in an appropriate manner. Put simply, your little citizens cannot act any kind of way or just say anything and expect the physical manifestation of the vision to become a reality. Why? A vision is heavily dependent on the right words been spoken (i.e., "I am smart!" etc.) and the appropriate behavior being displayed before the vision materializes into a present-time reality.

> *A vision has the unique ability to provoke the untapped potential that resides on the inside of the little citizen to rise to the surface.*

**4. Focus on the Possibilities.** Placing your attention on the possibilities keeps an individual and/or a group of people motivated while patiently waiting and consistently working towards the possibilities contained in the vision. Before I go any further, let me explain what I mean by the possibilities carried by the vision. An effective vision should always contain possibilities that will take an individual to another level. For example, the assigned vision for your community may be that all your little citizens are more considerate towards each other. The possibilities encapsulated in this particular vision are problem solving, effective communication, and teamwork.

However, the true bonus of focusing on the possibilities is on the leader, rather than the citizens. If the leader is negligent towards or resistant in acknowledging the possibilities of her citizens, how can the little citizens ever see or even recognize the possibilities they have a right to obtain? A customized vision that captures or acknowledges the needs of all its members will wean the people-centered leader from judgment and negative interactions with a child, which may be based on the leader's stereotypes or beliefs regarding the child's cultural background, home environment, and/or socioeconomic status. But in its purest form, you are to visualize not just one nor just a select few living out the possibilities carried within the vision, but rather all those who makeup the community. Emotional support has reached its fullest potential when no one feels left behind, but is included in the journey.

## Customizing Your Own Community Vision

Here are some simple steps you can take to customize your own vision for your community.

**Step 1.** Reflect and the write down where you want your community to be in six months to a year from now (if this is a home community, adjust the time frame from six months to two years from now).

**Step 2.** Reflect and write down what is hindering your community from excelling to another level. What is keeping your community in stagnation mode?

**Step 3.** Write the vision that describes the next level you desire for you and your little citizens to achieve in the near future.

**Step 4.** Within your vision, write down the goals and objectives that will take into consideration the overall developmental needs of all the citizens in your community. **Note:** One vision may not be enough to cover all the developmental needs of your community, so have another vision in place when one vision has been fulfilled.

**Step 5.** After the vision has be finalized, put it on a poster board or something with high visibility so that the whole community can see it and run with the vision—with your guidance of course.

*Your happiness should never be dependent upon what is or is not going on around you. Rather, your happiness should be the outcome of regularly employing an emotional state of joyfulness.*

# Reflections

# Reflections

# Reflections

# *Reflections*

*Happiness is a highly persuasive feeling. It ignites positive energy, which drives an individual or a group of people to do things they either would not normally do, not be willing to do, or be slow about doing.*

# Chapter 9

## A Happy Community

It is quite interesting how children nowadays have become proficient in being afraid, sad, anxious, and angry. But have children become proficient in being happy? Granted, we live in a time of wars and rumors of wars, hatred, violence, protesting, and political debates. These bombard the minds, emotions, and social interactions of those glued to their television, radio, and/or social media. It used to be, when sitting at a traffic light waiting for the light to turn green, you would hear different genres of music through the car window. Now, the majority of what you hear in passing is the news. May I add, the media would have you and me to believe that everyone—children included—are emotionally, socially, and mentally disarrayed, pacing the floor and endlessly twisting their fingers around their hair as a result of the current affairs of this world system. Something is definitely out of place when children are shortchanged in having a real childhood. It's a shame for them to be thrust into conflicting issues, circumstances, or crises that adults themselves find hard to handle.

Regardless of the times we live in, children should never be denied the privilege to enjoy the once-in-a-lifetime stage of childhood. Sheryl, isn't this chapter about having a happy community? I'm getting there! A happy community is where everyone is free to be who he is at that time and moment. Yes, children will experience hurts, disappointments, anxiety, frustrations, and even sadness, but these negative feelings should never become a permanent state of being for a child. Rather these are temporary conditions as he attempts to process the emotions that stem from unexpected, unwelcome events. In the process, he will gain a better understanding of life.

A people-centered leader who naturally projects happiness spearheads an emotionally supportive community. Also, she is cognizant of the emotional challenges a child (or children) may encounter on a daily basis. An emotionally supportive leader is purposefully driven to conduct group discussions and one-on-one conversations with the child's emotions in mind. She will also implement inspiring activities and music, not only to assist the child in learning and growing from life challenges, but also to teach them how to move on and embrace a healthier state of being, which will bring a joyful countenance.

## What Is Happiness?

If you had the opportunity to randomly select and interview people from all walks of life regarding their views on happiness, you would find no two views are the same. Happiness for one person is being with family and friends on special occasions, whereas happiness for another individual is having all his needs met. Both individual's views are relevant and correct, but they are based on the condition or situation at hand. If being happy were solely based on a favorable condition, then people would be governed by their emotions. Let me reveal some truth to you right now: your happiness should never be dependent upon what is or is not going on around you. Rather, your happiness should be the outcome of regularly employing an emotional state of joyfulness. Did you think being joyful and being happy were one and the same? No, they are not! Happiness is a feeling that is conditional, and being joyful is an emotional state of being, the byproduct of an inner knowing. Joy is the confidence an individual has about who he or she really is. Therefore, joy is constantly reflected before, in the middle of, and at the end of a positive or negative situation and/or event.

> *Regardless of the times we live in, children should never be denied the privilege to enjoy the once-in-a-lifetime stage of childhood.*

Happiness is the outer expression (or feeling) of being joyful. Now can you see the importance behind having the right word or words resonating throughout your community? By cultivating a stable identity amongst the members of your community, you help confirm not only who they are, but also what they are entitled to become, despite the opposition the little citizens may face in life. Having a strong sense of self ushers in the emotional state of joyfulness, which then is outwardly expressed through the little citizens' actions, verbal and non-verbal expressions, and conversations.

So happiness alone is not enough to substantiate a child's emotional state of being, simply because happiness is just a feeling that is based on the condition of one's environment. However, being happy can be a more frequent or natural response when a little citizen has been taught, through observation, how to respond to life's events and challenges from the standpoint of who he is (i.e., brave, strong, etc.) and the identity that has been cultivated inside of him. In other words, a child can be taught to draw from his or her inner strength. A child who is groomed to draw from the strength that exists within will always be more joyful than a child who depends on the outcome of his physical surroundings.

## Benefits of a Happy Community

A quick review: Happiness is the outer expression associated with being joyful.

Feeling happy should never be independent of being joyful because happiness alone is based on the condition of one's surroundings. In contrast, being joyful (emotion) is based on the solidity of one's identity. One's identity will always outweigh the condition of one's surroundings simply because one's surroundings constantly change. With that being said, let's look at the benefits of having a happy community in which the overall emotional state of your citizens is joyful.

*Your happiness should never be dependent upon what is or is not going on around you. Rather, your happiness should be the outcome of regularly employing an emotional state of joyfulness.*

## Benefits of a Happy Community

**1. Memorable Moments.** Children who are fortunate enough to be part of a happy community are encouraged to love, laugh, share, and enjoy the company of their fellow members (i.e., family members, friends, peers, etc.). Children who are taught through observation and practical application the art of positive social skills generate a euphoric environment that creates memorable moments. These moments become engraved on the canvas of the children's imaginations. The moment can be something as simple as designating time during the day to play positive, uplifting music for you and your little citizens to dance around the room, laughing and enjoying each other's company. I promise you this priceless activity will foster a happy countenance amongst you and your little citizens, thereby adding another joyful moment to their schema. Joyful moments stabilize the climate, or environment, of the community. A compilation of positive memories produces a photo album in a child's mind, allowing him to privately reminisce and also share with others.

**2. Increased Productivity.** Have you noticed when people are happy they are more cooperative? Happiness is a highly persuasive feeling that ignites positive energy and drives an individual or a group of people to do things that they either would not normally do or would be slow about doing. That is, happiness promotes productivity, which, in return, increases the social, emotional, mental, and physical health of a person. Children operating within a happy environment are more adventurous in learning and open to new concepts and ideas, all of which is beneficial to their academic achievement (McGhee, 2002). Education is not the only area of improvement. Children who are the product of a happy community also flourish in the following areas:

- Mentally, children are able to concentrate better and stay focused longer on what is being presented to them. This increases learning opportunities.

- Socially, children operating from a happy community are more open, not only learning positive social skills but also implementing the positive social skills acquired through observation.

- Emotionally, a happy community has a higher level of resilience due to fact that their leader and fellow peers are constantly supporting the little citizens when they are distressed. This support allows each citizen time to regroup and return back to the "set" emotional state of joyfulness.

**3. Laughter Is Medicine.** Finally, the third benefit of having a happy community is that it exhibits one of the traits of being happy: laughter. The physical component of a child's health is being appropriately addressed through laughter. Laughter is natural medicine for those who choose to partake of this natural remedy (McGhee, 2002). In addition, laughter releases feel-good hormones, endorphins, which are well known for enhancing one's mood. Therefore, laughter fosters an overall sense of emotional, social, physical, and mental wellness.

## Promoting Happiness in Your Community

Here are a few simple activities you can add to your arsenal to promote happiness throughout your community.

**Make Me Laugh.** This fun-filled activity can be done either one-on-one or collectively as a group. Each participant is given the opportunity to make a funny expression or sound until the other person starts to laugh. Keep rotating the participants until everyone has the opportunity to make someone laugh.

---

*Happiness is a highly persuasive feeling that ignites positive energy and drives an individual or a group of people to do things that they either would not normally do or would be slow about doing.*

---

**Story Time.** Utilize age-appropriate books with emotionally based scenarios that will challenge the little citizens to participate in an open discussion. This discussion will allow them to share their opinions regarding the emotional state of the character being displayed in the book. Recommended books are as follows: *Happy Hippo, Angry Duck: Book of Moods* by Sandra Boynton; *How to Be Happy* by Eleanor Davis; *Dealing with Feeling Happy* by Isabel Thomas.

**Let's Dance.** Music is a universal language that touches the heart of people like no other medium can. Music inspires a rhythmic movement in a person and generates positive energy. Playing joyful, uplifting music allows your little citizens to dance freely while the feel-good hormones, endorphins, are being released in their bodies, creating positive energy.

Not just any kind of music should be introduced to a child's ear gate, but rather music that is filled with substance, filled with encouraging words. Use music that will saturate the canvas of the child's imagination with pleasant thoughts.
I would recommend the following songs from the Super Fun Show musical library (superfunshow.com) to set the atmosphere in your community: *Born to Win; It's a Happy Day; Brave, Strong, Champion; I Like That.* There is nothing better than your little citizens constantly being refreshed with words of encouragement.

# Reflections

# *Reflections*

# Reflections

*Positive peer relationships are at their best when a group of people not only gets along, but also learns from each other as they explore their surroundings.*

## Can We All Get Along?

### Peer Relationships

Developing an emotionally supportive community definitely takes time and patience, especially when your community consists of various personalities, cultural backgrounds, social circumstances, and emotional levels. No child enters into your community as a perfect being. There are some children who easily adapt to their environment, both socially and emotionally; there are other children who may have difficulties with interpersonal skills and/or who may be emotionally fragile when with their peers, or even with people in general. Whatever the social and emotional makeup of your community, learning how to get along with each other is the key to a strong and successful community. The fabric of the community is based on unity and built on positive peer relationships. Harmony is the heartbeat of the community as the little citizens explore, learn, and grow. Positive peer relationships are at their best when a group of people not only gets along, but also learns from each other as they explore their surroundings. Positive peer relationships are most definitely a vital tool for developing an emotionally supportive community.

## Defining Positive Peer Relationships

Positive peer relation is stimulating social intertwining that consistently propagates genuine and authentic connectedness between the children in the community. A strong sense of belonging that fosters social, mental, physical and emotional wellness for everyone.

*Developing an emotionally supportive community definitely takes time and patience, especially when your community consists of various personalities, cultural backgrounds, social circumstances, and emotional levels.*

## The Purpose of Positive Peer Relationships

**Purpose #1. Give and Receive.** When it comes to stimulating social interaction and positive peer relationships, there is a give and receive exchange, both verbal and nonverbal, that is constantly taking place amongst those who participate. This social exchange is at its best when the participants, in this case the little citizens, are being people-centered, as opposed to being self-centered. Self-centeredness, or what I call "it's-all-about-me syndrome," will cause the fabric of the community to become unraveled, thereby preventing the little citizens from having the opportunity to experience the give and receive exchange. So what is the give and receive exchange? The give and receive exchange is basically knowing when to give of one's self through listening, sharing, and helping when needed and when to receive, giving the other person a chance to give.

**Purpose #2. Ownership.** The longevity of a community is based on its members taking ownership of the community. Continuously reinforcing positive peer relationships through social-emotional activities and/or properly intervening when little citizens are at odds with each other sends a strong and compelling message that it is perfectly ok to take ownership of the community, both personally and collectively. Children who have a solid sense of belonging in their community display the following traits:

- Increased communication skills, able to verbally express feelings, likes and dislikes, and share one's opinions.

- A sense of fullness as he enjoys the benefits or special privileges available to those who are members of the community.

- Admirable behavior and words that uphold the reputation of the community.

When I have the honor to conduct parent/child rallies with my husband, I remind parents that children are a reflection of the parents when they venture outside of their home environment. A child will experience a strong sense of belonging when his parents not only effectively model appropriate social and emotional skills, but also consistently maintain a loving and nurturing home environment. By having a strong sense of belonging in his primary community, the home, the little citizen becomes faithful in upholding the reputation of his home environment when he is in the presence of others, be it at school, church, and/or other external communities.

**Purpose #3. Advanced Social Skills.** The third purpose of positive peer relationships is for the little citizen to learn durable social skills that are capable of preparing him for unexpected turbulence or obstacles. As our little citizen engages in what we call life, he needs to be socially advanced in order to effectively address the challenges, learn from the experiences, and move on to the next phase in life.

By constantly challenging your little citizens to learn new social skills and by putting these skills into use via activities and/or revisiting past interactions, the child's arsenal of skills will keep expanding for future reference.

**Purpose #4. Looking beyond Self.** Anytime you are amongst people, there is a part of the self that is emotionally, socially, mentally, or even physically compromised. For instance, when you go to a crowded mall, with wall-to-wall people, especially on the holidays, your personal space is comprised more often than not. There is a part of the self that has to be sacrificed, either for the sake of others or for personal gain. Positive peer relationships are all about give and take.

*A very touching moment in my husband's life occurred when his father passed away in 2004. The advice he received from a friend was to go to work in an effort to keep his mind occupied.*

*Positive peer relationships already permeated in this particular community. The little citizens were sensitive enough to know that my husband was going through something, without knowing exactly what he was going through. The citizens of the community were emotionally connected to Shawn during his time of bereavement. One by one, the little citizens came and gave my husband a hug during an enrichment program at the school. This is giving of one's self at its best! Looking beyond self compels the little citizen to freely give and to freely receive from others. Combining the two responses (giving and receiving), you have what I refer to as reliable emotional support.*

## Types of Members in the Community

No community is perfect, but the leader and the citizens should be striving for perfection. A strong and successful community does not come to fruition overnight, for the simple reason that all the members of the community are at different levels socially and emotionally; therefore, children must be met where they are in order to coach them to the next level of maturity. So let's explore the different types of citizens that possibly exist in your community.

**The Distancer:** This member is more of a loner than a social butterfly. His or her social and emotional development is stifled, due to either the child's lack of interest in socializing or his confidence in taking the plunge and engaging with peers. Children who are socially and emotionally cut off from the community may appear to be uninterested, but do not be fooled. They are quite aware of what is going on around them. Distancers are, indeed, socially and emotionally engaged with their community through their visual and auditory senses, and sometimes even through their actions.

**How to Meet a Distancer Where She Is:** Children who are socially or emotionally distant need the leader to do what I call the "social-emotional waltz" with them. This means you let the Distancer lead, through physical actions, as she makes three steps into the community to mingle with fellow peers, participate in extracurricular or educational activities, and/or seek comfort. You make three steps by celebrating her and making it a big deal as the Distancer attempts to execute social skills to the best of her abilities. In addition, make sure she gets the most out of each and every activity/lesson being implemented during that window of opportunity.

Children who often distance themselves socially and emotionally from the affairs of the community have a better chance of coming out of their shell when there is a happy medium found between the child's efforts and the leader's support system. By both parties (little citizen and people-centered leader) consistently participating in the social-emotional waltz, the leader of the community becomes more patient, creative, and sensitive to the needs of the child, and the little citizen gradually becomes socially and emotionally engaged, more trusting towards others, and more confident in self.

**Social Butterfly:** For this type of member, it comes naturally for him or her to interact with others. It appears that he finds enjoyment being in the presence of others, and as a result, his social and emotional skills are constantly being put to use for the betterment of self and others. Even though a Social Butterfly adds a certain flavor to the social-emotional dimension of the community, there are still some minor interpersonal relationship adjustments that have to be made in order for your little Social Butterfly to blossom into a well-rounded citizen.

**Adjustment 1: Too Chatty.** Children who display advanced social skills at an early age are rarely at a loss for words. They are like the rabbit on the Energizer commercial; they can go on and on and on. Although it is quite nice to hear children use their words, some children can be overbearing to the point that they drown out everyone else, thereby depriving others of the opportunity to practice using their social and emotional skills.

The Social Butterfly means well. It's just that he either has not been properly taught or has not quite grasped the concept of being considerate of others when conversing.

**Adjustment 2: Being a Good Listener.** Let's be real. Having a Social Butterfly (or butterflies) in your community can be overwhelming at times. How? Children who are more socially engaged than others are oftentimes better talkers than listeners. As a result, they may be hearing what you say, but are they really listening? Social Butterflies are so caught up with their opinions, thoughts, and "social world" that doing what they are told and paying attention takes second place.

**Adjustment 3: Stepping over Social Boundaries.** Do you remember the old expression, "Too many chiefs and not enough Indians"? It simply means that too many people want to be leaders, but very few people want to be followers. What I draw from this famous expression is that boundaries become less significant when all the chiefs are in competition with each other, with no limitations or boundaries amongst them when obtaining the position of head chief. Children, on the other hand, are not out for becoming the head chief, but you will find that the little citizens are competitive when it comes wanting to be heard and/or needing you all to themselves. As a result of this innocent competitiveness, children can step over social boundaries, clueless as to what they have just done. Your Social Butterfly oftentimes—let me take that back, a lot of times—will step over boundaries and slip into the role of an adult, either a parent or teacher (depending on the type the community you oversee, home or school). In other words, their advanced social skills can interfere with the social, emotional, academic, and moral impartation you need and want to deposit into the lives of each and every little citizen. If the Social Butterfly of your community is not properly directed on the boundaries for being attentive during instructional learning, being respectful towards others when it is their turn to talk, and/or following instructions when given, this will eventually cause the boundaries of your community to become enmeshed and weak.

**How to Meet a Social Butterfly Where He Is:** Just like butterfly species are beautiful, yet gentle, so are the little Social Butterflies in your community. A socially advanced citizen has so much inside that he wants and needs to express. If a leader is insensitive, impatient, or harsh in her approach (i.e., separating the socially inclined from the rest of his peers by sitting him at a table by himself, etc.), trying to keep the Social Butterfly contained in a bubble, it will eventually suppress the child's enthusiasm to execute his social skills. Because the little citizen's spirit is crushed when you separate him from the daily affairs of the community, you may observe the following signs:

- Loss of interest in attending the community (i.e., school, etc.)
- Daydreaming
- Lack of interest in participating in community activities
- Decrease in peer interaction
- Sadness
- Decrease in academic performance

## Pass It On

So that you can meet the little citizen where he is, this simple technique, "pass it on," will assist you in regulating order when dialogue is being exchanged amongst the members of your community. In addition, this social activity helps promote social etiquettes, which challenges the Social Butterfly to be mindful in honoring the rules associated with taking turns when expressing one's opinion, sharing one's experiences, and/or responding to a question.

Pass it on helps a Social Butterfly to develop a listening ear, patience, and consideration for others, which over time weakens the strong undertones of self-centeredness. This technique can be implemented either during a one-on-one interaction or during a group activity, but it is most effective during group conversation. The material needed is a soft object, such as a squeeze ball or a foam baton. The soft object serves as a conductor that controls the flow of the conversation amongst the little citizens. Whoever has the squeeze ball or the baton in his or her hands is the one who has the floor to talk while the other members listen attentively. Once the child has finished his statement, the leader selects another little citizen to speak, and the ball or baton is passed on accordingly. **Note:** If a child (or children) is being disrespectful while another child is speaking, the leader will make a subtle comment, such as, "I like how Tommie recognizes that Sara has the baton in her hand, and he is listening attentively as she speaks."

**The Little Enforcer:** We all have one. Some people call him or her a bully; others may call him a troublemaker. I call him the Little Enforcer. The Little Enforcer is more aggressive than his peers when it comes to exerting his social and emotional skills. Even though his intentions are not to cause harm to anyone, there is a boldness about him that is driven by his desire to have or to be. This drive makes him somewhat pushy, thereby bringing discomfort to those around him.

For example, Johnny is three and quite big for his age. Johnny is socially aggressive when it comes to making friends. In an effort to make friends, Johnny oftentimes barges in and scrambles the social flow among his peers while they are playing ball. Rather than asking if can he play or waiting to be invited to play, Johnny forces himself on his peers by taking the ball and throwing it to one of the little citizens, as if he had been playing with them along. His peers are intimidated by his size and do not have the courage to tell him that he cannot play. As a result, some of his peers go along with the new flow and play with Johnny, while others run away crying, going to tell the leader what just happened. Poor little Johnny; all he wanted was to make friends and play.

**How to Meet the Little Enforcer Where He Is:** First and foremost, you must realize that children do not acquire social or emotional skills on their own. Rather, their social and emotional skills are a reflection of the interaction patterns taking place within their family system. Not all social and emotional skills that are "homegrown" are appropriate for public. Some families have strong social skills, which may be intimidating or too aggressive for others. As a result, the Little Enforcer must be taught, through reenactment role-playing and through scenarios and/or books centered around appropriate social and emotional development, how to tone down his forcefulness and cooperate with the set rules of the community that are centered around peer relationships. He must see these rules can guide him to achieve his social desires (i.e., establishing friendship, having a turn to play with a toy, etc.). In other words, it is vital that the child learn that it is a joint venture when it comes to establishing positive peer relationships—not a solo act.

**Check on Your Fellow Peer:** This technique puts the Little Enforcer in someone else's shoes. The leader assigns the Little Enforcer as her helper to check on fellow citizens who are experiencing disappointments, hurts, and/or difficulties as they participate in the daily community activities. In essence, the Little Enforcer becomes the big brother or sister who makes sure everyone is all right. This technique not only makes the child less aggressive socially, but also causes him to be empathetic towards others, thereby appropriately strengthening his emotional skills.

**We're Stuck: What Can We Do?** The last technique I would like to present to you will help the child develop his problem-solving skills. Select situations currently taking place that will provide the most learning opportunities as it relates to socio-emotional development. Then explain to the little citizens that we are stuck in this situation. Ask them, "What can we do to get out of it?"

Do not solve the problem for them, but rather coach them along the way. It will allow them to get more out of the experience when their problem-solving skills are put to work. For example, Sara snatched the ball from Melody and walked away. Bring all the members involved together and tell them, "We are stuck in this situation and need to get out." Give them (both Sara and Melody) clues (i.e., the social rules of the community) on the appropriate social and emotional skills needed to use in order to get out of the stuck mode.

---

### *Children must be met where they are in order to coach them to the next level of maturity*

---

**The Whiner:** This type of citizen, a Whiner, is a complainer who can never be satisfied. Something is always wrong: "My food is too hot!"; "Someone moved my chair!"; "He is sitting too close to me!"; "I want Cheez-Its and not cheese balls!" On and on, the Whiner expresses his discontentment with his environment to the point that he forfeits his opportunity to advance socially and emotionally. You cannot blame the little citizen for his social and emotional deficiencies because he is a reflection of his home environment. I am trying to be nice, but what I really want to say is that he learned this annoying behavior from one of his parents who whines. Behaviors are learned and then emulated once mastered.

If this behavior is not properly addressed, it can eventually put a damper on things as it relates to positive peer relationships. In addition, other little citizens will start mimicking this negative behavior. A community filled with Whiners is definitely not a good thing.

**How to Meet the Whiner Where He Is (Find the Good):** Meeting a Whiner where he is and then taking him beyond being a complainer or a dissatisfied little citizen is a job. It will take time, patience, and consistency, but transforming a Whiner into a happy little citizen is worth its weight in gold. I love this technique, find the good, simply because it challenges the Whiner to look for the good in a situation rather than the bad. For instance, the Whiner complains about his chair being moved; you help find the good in this situation by reminding him that at least he has a chair to call his own. Constantly reminding the Whiner to find the good in a thing or situation will assist the child in reprogramming his way of thinking from always seeing the bad to seeing the good. This allows the child to shift his emotions from connecting with the negative to embracing the positive. Over time, your Whiner will transform into a cheerful delight who enjoys his surroundings.

**The Ideal Little Citizen:** Every leader desires this type of citizen or citizens in her community. The Ideal Little Citizen's social and emotional skills are exceptional and to be admired by his or her peers. The number of times this particular child experiences any social discrepancies or emotional meltdowns can be counted on one hand, if at all. Why? They are, for the most part, in sync with the set rules established for positive peer relationships.

*I once came in contact with a little girl at the gym who would be an ideal citizen for any respectful community out there. I went to the bathroom at the gym before leaving for my next destination. I was running late for my hair appointment. Ladies, how many of you know that it is a no-no to be late for a hair appointment because someone can take your place and then you will have to wait? Well, anyway, back to my story! I was running late and in a rush. I had no reason to look down, but in the midst of rushing to leave the gym, I almost ran over a little girl with beautiful blue eyes. She looked up at me with her beautiful smile, and while eating her Cheerios, she said, "Excuse Me!" She did not cry or appear frightened, but rather she kept her composure. I told her mom, who was close by, that she was doing a good job with her daughter, and she replied, "It is my responsibility to make sure that my child is well mannered toward all she comes in contact with." Wow! The fruit (the child's social and emotional skills) does not fall far from the tree (the mother's social and emotional skills). Children become who you are.*

## Keep Imparting

So how do you grow an Ideal Little Citizen? Where they are? It's simple. Keep imparting social and emotional skills that will take him or her to the next level, both on an interpersonal and intrapersonal level. Children do not come into this world knowing everything. They are always learning to live what we call life. And as they learn, their arsenal is filled with skills that help them to become productive little citizens.

## Conclusion

Positive peer relationships are a masterpiece in the making when you encourage your little citizens to learn and grow together, in the good times and also during the not so good times. For every challenge, there is a lesson to learn.

# Reflections

# Reflections

# Reflections

# Chapter 11

## The Interpreter

*Matthew was six-years-old when his mother died. His mother left the house one evening to go the hospital to address some health problems she was experiencing, but unfortunately, she never returned home. If that was not enough, funeral services and the burial came and went—all without Matthew attending or being able to say farewell to the mother he loved so dearly. Maybe the family members were trying to shelter him from the hurt and pain of his mother's death, or maybe his mother's final wishes were for Matthew not to attend the funeral because she only wanted him to remember her alive. In either case, the woman who birthed him, loved him, protected him, and nurtured him was no longer a physical reality, but only a memory. Clueless to all that was going on, Matthew increasingly became emotionally distressed. There were many unknowns for him, and he was unable to understand his overwhelming emotions. He was desperately in need of an interpreter who could translate what his emotions were trying to convey to those around him.*

Pause! There is more of this story to be told. But I would like for this statement to resonate in your heart and mind as you read this particular chapter: children are resilient, but they are not machines. I know this is a strong statement, but we oftentimes take for granted the resilience of children. It is, indeed, easy for them to bounce back and pick up where they left off when minor upsets occur. Yes, there are even children who have shown high resilience in the most crippling environment or in the most calamitous event. However, if children remain in a hopeless environment, without ever receiving counseling or proper emotional support, they will most likely carry baggage into their adulthood. This emotional baggage will produce negative social, emotional, mental, and behavioral patterns.

What we fail to realize is that children are not machines that we quickly fix and immediately put back to use. Rather, children are human beings with real feelings and emotions that need to be properly addressed—not brushed off—in order for the child to move on in life.

As a people-centered leader, you will find that you are constantly wearing new hats as you lead your little citizens from one level of development (socially, emotionally, mentally, academically, physically, and morally) to the next. So if you do not mind, I would like to introduce to you a new hat (role) you can add to your arsenal; this new hat is that of an interpreter.

## The Interpreter

An interpreter is one who translates the emotions that are being showcased or communicated through the child's physical actions (i.e., hitting, crying, social isolation, etc.). An interpreter is cognizant of the primary emotional state that is displayed by a child, both positive and negative. She realizes the emotion (or emotions) stems from some thought or thoughts which are associated with a past or present event. The interpreter also recognizes that it is not enough to just identify the emotion that is being displayed through the child's physical actions, but the interpreter is prepared to do some detective work to determine the underlying cause or causes for a particular emotion being activated.

## *Children are resilient, but they are not machines.*

### The Purpose of an Interpreter

The purpose of your role as an interpreter is three-fold:

1.  As the interpreter of your community, the little citizens heavily depend on you to resolve what they may be experiencing. Whether they are not feeling well, being bullied by their peers, grieving over a death of a loved one or pet, or being physically or emotionally abused by an adult figure, the trauma brings everything to a halt until what they are communicating to you is clearly heard and resolved.

2.  The second purpose for being the interpreter is that you can bring comfort to your little citizens as they know they are being emotionally supported when they are happy and even when they are distressed. Being supported by your leader, the interpreter, is comforting to the child. He knows he can express what he is going through, trusting you will interpret what he is trying to communicate to you. He trusts that you will also develop a plan to help him get over the hurdle and focus on becoming a stronger and better little citizen.

3.  Finally, the third purpose of your role as an interpreter is to assist the child in obtaining closure to whatever has been distressing him emotionally. True closure can only occur when the little citizen has had the opportunity to experience the following:

a) An inner knowing that he has truly been heard and understood.
b) The ability to process emotions and feelings through helpful techniques/activities and to learn alternative behavior and thought patterns, especially if old thoughts and behavioral patterns are harmful to self and others.
c) Clarity in what he is going through.
d) The ability to either say or physically demonstrate that he is ready to move on (In other words, the child is back in the thriving mode.)

Let's connect the steps of proper closure to the conclusion of my story regarding Matthew. *Matthew was quickly slipping into a depressed state, and it was becoming quite apparent in his performance at school and his social interactions with others, both at home and school. It was as if everyone had moved on, and he was stuck in the past, in hopes of his mother returning home to him so that he could get back in the flow with his rhythm of life. Those who knew Matthew understood his dilemma and sympathized with him, but they were all missing one key element: they failed to interpret what he was trying to communicate through his emotions. Matthew was speaking all along, but it was through his emotions, rather than with actual words.*

*One day his aunt, who was given custody over Matthew, realized that her nephew desperately needed counseling. As a result, she took him to a local behavior health clinic for children. The children's therapist assigned to Matthew was known for her unique ability to create therapeutic interventions to get clients to communicate their emotions and feelings. In addition, she also gave them alternative ways to express and process what they were internally combating.*

*During one of his sessions, she provided construction paper and crayons for Matthew to express what he was thinking and feeling regarding his mother's death. He was quite occupied and appeared to be very content, even relieved, while drawing. It appeared the therapist was able to tap into what Matthew was trying to communicate the whole time. Matthew drew a picture of a sun and clouds with his mother nestled within the clouds, looking down at him. The therapist had Matthew talk about his picture. He quickly responded that his mom was now in heaven and she was happy. The expression on his face was priceless; the therapist felt a warm feeling come over her.*

*An interpreter is one who translates the emotions that are being showcased or communicated through the child's physical actions.*

*After several sessions, the therapist finally thought it was time for her and Matthew to participate in a memorial service for his mom. Remember that Matthew was unable to attend the funeral conducted for his mother. The therapist had Matthew create a card for his mother and insert words to express how much he loved her and missed her. After getting permission from the aunt, the therapist went to the store to purchase some colorful helium balloons, engraved with fancy writing saying, "I love you and miss you!" Shortly after, she drove to Matthew's home and picked him up, and then they headed off to the cemetery. This cemetery was beautiful and well-manicured. Tall trees full of leaves stood in each section of the cemetery. As the wind was gently blowing and the sun was beaming down on them, there was just enough heat to keep them warm on that cold winter day.*

*Matthew tightly held the therapist's hand as they walked around and viewed the different gravesites. As they finally approached the grave that he had been longing to visit, Matthew asked the big question: "How did my mother get down there?" The therapist took a deep breath and described the burial procedure in its simplest form to her client. A child who had been silent for months suddenly spoke many questions. After all questions were answered, the therapist had Matthew read aloud the card he had made his mom. Then he securely placed it on the gravesite. The therapist softly sang the beautiful song, "You Are So Beautiful to Me." As they walked back to the car, the therapist noticed that Matthew was smiling. Matthew finally had closure regarding his mother's death. Even though his mother would be just a memory to others, he believed deep within his heart that his mother was looking down at him to make sure her little Matthew was ok. The therapist, the interpreter, took Matthew out for ice cream. Then she took the socially, emotionally, and mentally renewed Matthew back home to be reunited with his family.*

## Having a Course of Action

Overseeing a community that consists of little citizens can be quite overwhelming sometimes, particularly when your little citizens are constantly in discovery mode when it comes to their emotions and feelings. You will find that children's emotional responses to a situation and/or event are not all the same; therefore, each child should be handled on an individual basis. As a leader, you will need a course of action, a plan to effectively interpret what emotion a child is trying to communicate to you through his physical actions.

Consider the steps below:

1.  List the contributing factors that may be associated with the little citizen being emotionally distressed. I suggest you have at least three or four contributing factors to explore until you find the main reason behind the child's sudden change in behavior or the cause of his dysfunctional/inappropriate behavioral patterns. For example, Grant, age three, has been soiling his pants for the past two weeks and becoming socially withdrawn from his peers. Probable causes associated with Grant soiling his pants are being bullied by his peers; a physical ailment that requires medical attention; reoccurrence of a tragic event; and physical and/or sexual abuse. **Note:** It is not uncommon for children who either have been bullied and/or physically or sexually abused to regress back to their infant stage of life by soiling.

2. Once the contributing factor or factors have been determined, write down a list, if needed, of the impact the child's sudden behavior change or ongoing negative behavioral pattern will have on the other members of the community. For instance, Grant suddenly soiling in his pants could possibly cause him to be teased by his peers, which could possibly put a damper on his positive peer relationships in the community.

3. The last step is being sensitive towards the child by creating a plan of action to properly address what is causing him to be emotionally distressed. The goal here is to get the child back into rhythm with the emotional and social climate of the community. For example, you might be more observant of the interpersonal relationships (i.e., during play time, etc.) Grant has with his peers. Observe whether there are signs of bullying being displayed by his peers that could cause Grant to regress both physically and socially. Or, during story time, read a book that sends a message to all the little citizens that bullying is wrong, and then allow the children to give their opinions accordingly. Or, have a meeting with Grant's parents to discuss your findings and recommend that he should visit the doctor for medical evaluation and to receive proper medical treatment.

In closing, the hat of an interpreter is invaluable when it comes to understanding how a child communicates when he or she is emotionally perturbed. The people-centered leader always makes sure that all of his or her members are heard—even when they are communicating without words. Remember, children communicate through their emotions until they begin to advance in their social skills and language development. Until then, just watch; their behavior will tell you what is going on.

# Reflections

# Reflections

*Every child needs and wants to be loved, respected, valued, remembered, and understood as he journeys through life, discovering who he is.*

# Chapter 12

## The Supporter

Another key element for developing an emotionally supportive community is being an advocate or a supporter for those you oversee as they journey through life to discover who they are. It is during this exploration that there will be a mixture of emotions as they try to make sense of the victories and obstacles they may face in life. We sometimes, as adults, take for granted that because they are children, what they experience in life is minor. I am here to tell you, no one on this earth is exempt from life's challenges—no matter how young, old, or in-between he is.

There are many challenges a child may face: Daniel is having a difficult time in mastering a particular concept at school; no one wants to be Breanna's friend; Brian's parents are in the process of getting a divorce, so instead of having one residence to live in, he will have two. The list can go on and on, but the point I want to get across is this: regardless of the challenges your little citizens may be going through while under your watch, they desperately are in need of a leader who not only acknowledges but supports the fact that every child needs and wants to be loved, respected, remembered, understood, and valued—even in the most uncomfortable, bewildering, and alarming times in their life. Having someone support them when they are going through difficulties (and even when things are going well) will help them get over the hurdles in life so that they can move forward.

## The Three Phases

It was never meant for anyone to be stuck in adversity, but rather to go through adversity and come out at the other end stronger and wiser. How many of you know people who appear to be perpetually going through adversity and rarely, if at all, coming out on the other side? They are stuck! Their emotions and thoughts are so enmeshed with the adversity that they are unable to see the light at the end of the tunnel. This helpless state of being is not only unhealthy, but it can also lessen an individual's will to thrive in life.

There are three phases an individual, in this case, a little citizen, will experience when faced with adversity. The initial phase is what I call the "arrival," or the onset, of the challenge or adversity. This is when the challenge presents itself to the individual (child) and his or her thoughts begin to process what has just taken place. Next, his emotions are sorted through until the right one is selected for the situation at hand. For example, Sara was the only child until her life was disrupted (the challenge) by the arrival of newly born baby brother. Sara started to process in her mind how she was going to be neglected and loved less by her parents because they were going to be consumed with taking care of her baby brother. As Sara continued to subject herself to these irrational thoughts, the emotion that was selected was sadness, and it was physically expressed by refusing to go to school and by wetting herself.

**The Supporter's Role in Phase I: The Arrival Phase.** The role of the supporter during the initial onset of a challenge, crisis, or adversity is to let the child know that she is not alone and that you, the supporter, sympathizes with what she is feeling regarding her most recent dethronement. This phase consists of a lot of listening and hugs, so be ready to give both. In the example provided above, the leader would hold Sara (or give her a hug or a gentle pat on the back) if needed and let her know that he knows what the child is going through. General disclosure of the leader's past experience can be provided if it relates to what the child is currently experiencing. The purpose of general disclosure is so that the child knows she is not the only one who has felt dethroned.

> *It is during this exploration that there will be a mixture of emotions as they try to make sense of the victories and obstacles they may face in life.*

**The Supporter's Role in Phase II: In the Midst of a Challenge.** The second phase of a challenge is what I call "in the midst of." This is when the negative feelings and emotions that have enmeshed or intertwined with the challenge need to be detached from the challenge so that the child can get through the challenge and move forward in life. For instance, Sara appears to be somewhat stuck in her dilemma. She is having a difficult time in separating from the negative emotions associated with being dethroned by her baby brother; as a result, her emotional disposition has affected her performance at school.

During "in the midst of" a challenge, the role of a supporter shifts from being a listener and consoler to an encourager and mentor. As I indicated earlier, it was never meant for anyone to be stuck in adversity or challenge, but rather to go through and come out stronger and wiser. But what happens when a person becomes weary, frustrated, discouraged, lost, or confused while in the midst of the challenge? The easy route would be to do nothing and succumb to whatever the adversity unleashes, in hopes that it will come to an end one day. However, this plan of action will only leave a person physically and mentally drained, thereby preventing him from seeing beyond the challenge. The inability to see beyond where you are now leads to nowhere.

Never encourage your little citizens to avoid the inevitable, the challenges of life, but do encourage them to face the challenge head-on because there is a revelation, a newness, or an unknown truth about themselves that will be discovered during their time of discomfort. In other words, going through the challenge will bring to surface new little citizens who are wiser, stronger, and more confident, children who are socially, emotionally, and mentally mature. So the next time a challenge unexpectedly visits one of your little citizens, he will have experience under his belt and a plan to access during the arduous times in life. Awkward as this may sound, life's challenges, if faced head-on, can increase a child's problem-solving skills and social and emotional skills.

All those who are currently facing a challenge in life should exemplify an eagle. This amazing bird does not avoid a storm, but rather flies directly into the storm, knowing that the wind blowing to move the storm will pop the eagle above the storm. Not only can an eagle fly twice as fast in a storm, but also the eagle is growing stronger while in the midst of the storm.

And so it is with children. Being in the midst of a challenge requires forward movement, movement that requires an individual to get back in the ring as a contender and face the challenge with the intention to win. The supporter role as an encourager is to provide uplifting words that will resound more loudly than the challenge itself, thereby causing the little citizen to reflect more on the words being spoken oven him than the obstacle. Being encouraged, he can then direct his attention to moving forward, rather than staying stuck in the situation.

Any time one of your little citizens is experiencing a challenging time in his life, he is going to need a mentor to assist him in navigating his way through the challenge. You can help him replace the old thought with new thoughts that are more solution based; you can encourage him to adopt alternative behavior patterns that help him embrace and work through the challenge at hand; and you can help him establish obtainable goals that allow him to see the change and progress taking place while in the midst of the challenge. In short, everything a supporter does when operating in his or her role as a mentor is to guide the child through the challenge, and once he has conquered the challenge, assist him in getting back on course towards being a productive little citizen.

**The Supporter's Role in Phase III: Coming Out.** The third phase of a challenge is the conclusion, or what I call "coming out." This is when the individual, the little citizen, has successfully triumphed over a challenge in life, and as a result, he came out more mature and confident in his ability to deal with life. During this phase, the supporter's role shifts from an encourager and mentor to a cheerleader and reflector.

> *Life's challenges, if faced head-on, can increase a child's problem-solving skills and social and emotional skills.*

Successfully overcoming a challenge should never be taken lightly, but rather a celebration is definitely in order for those who stood the test, as opposed to throwing in the towel. Our little ones, especially, should be commended for their acts of bravery every time they defeat life's challenges. Having a cheering section waiting as the child exits the challenge becomes a confidence booster that reassures him of what he is capable of being and doing—even in the most uncomfortable circumstances. The supporter role as cheerleader is to lavish the little citizen with positive words and statements (i.e., " I am so proud of you!"; "You did it!"), which confirm the victory over the challenge.

A challenge is not to be viewed as a mere experience that is soon forgotten once an individual's thoughts, emotions, and physical health have been exercised by its demands. Rather, there should be times of reflection in which an individual steps back and examines what he or she came through. It is what I call a "back-then and right-now moment." These call for the supporter to operate in her role as a reflector who aids the little citizen in mentally revisiting the event (the back-then moment) and reflecting on what he was before the challenge and what he has now become (or what he is capable of doing) after the challenge (the right-now moment). The reflector highlights the achievements, sacrifices, and strides the child has made to be where he is now.

## Becoming Who He Needed Her to Be

*I recall hearing a story about a little boy by the name of Jason. He was six-years-old, going on seven. Jason was clinically diagnosed with manic depression (Bipolar I), along with ADHD. His mother would periodically abandon Jason and his two other siblings as she ventured off to live the wild life with her various boyfriends. His mother was heavily addicted to methamphetamine. As a result, Jason's maternal grandparents were eventually granted legal custody over Jason and his two other siblings. Jason's academic performance and conduct suffered mainly because of his longing for a stable relationship with his mother, but he also needed his medication to be properly adjusted to combat his emotional swings.*

*As you can well see, Jason had a lot of things going on in his life. You could say he was facing the challenges of life. Jason was perpetually going through adversity, but rarely coming out. He was stuck! And as a result, his emotions and thoughts were becoming enmeshed with this never-ending cycle. Jason desperately needed a supportive mentor to help him both see and experience something different in life. Jason needed hope in his world in order to thrive and move forward.*

*You remember the therapist who was the interpreter for Matthew in chapter 11? Well, this same therapist became the supporter for Jason. One day she was called to the school where Jason attended. When the therapist arrived to his class-room, she noted the teacher appeared quite frustrated and anxious. The teacher immediately charged in on the therapist regarding Jason's disruptive behavior and his inability to complete his work. The teacher insisted Jason's behavior was becoming too overwhelming to handle. The therapist quietly listened, and then she gently took Jason's hand and led him outside. It was quite obvious the teacher could not provide this little citizen the support he needed; therefore, the therapist had to intervene.*

*When the therapist took Jason outside, she could sense something was wrong. Out of nowhere, Jason started to cry, and the therapist immediately picked him up, and he rested his head on her shoulder for comfort. The therapist was trying to maintain her balance as she was holding Jason. Jason was a big boy! But it did not matter, the therapist could feel that Jason was emotionally and mentally tired. He was fed up with being entangled in this ongoing cycle of despair and needed some relief. What Jason needed was a mother figure to console him in his time of need. While still holding Jason, whose head rested on her shoulder and whose legs were wrapped around her waist, the therapist, the supporter, the consoler, the sympathizer, found a place to sit. As she held Jason, she began to rock him as if he were a newborn baby. She began to sing a beautiful song filled with words of encouragement. All of a sudden, Jason's body began to relax as if he did not have a care in the world. While the therapist and Jason were relishing this moment, the sun was beaming down on the both of them as if to say everything is going to be all right.*

*That was a pivotal moment, in both the therapist's and Jason's life. From that moment on, the therapist helped Jason not only face various challenges in his life, but also to come out at the other end wiser, stronger, and more confident in himself. All he needed was a supporter who could love him, value him, remember him, respect him, and understand him.*

# Reflections

# Reflections

*Maintaining the mind in a productive mode will stimulate positive emotions and feelings, generate positive energy, and spark creativity; in contrast, being idle-minded brings negative and irrelevant thoughts, thereby stimulating negative emotions and feelings, negative energy, and no creativity.*

# Chapter 13

## Occupied Mind, Positive Emotions

Productive little citizens are happy little citizens. Productivity in and of itself is a sure sign that your little citizens' minds are occupied and their emotions and feelings are in harmony with their thoughts. In other words, maintaining the mind in a productive mode will stimulate positive emotions and feelings, generate positive energy, and spark creativity; in contrast, being idle-minded brings negative and irrelevant thoughts, thereby stimulating negative emotions and feelings, negative energy, and no creativity. People have an inner desire to be occupied (Raghunathan, 2011). In being busy, an individual is happy and more prone to maintain a positive emotional state. I heard someone say that people function best when they are happy.

An emotionally supportive community is all about allowing the children to explore their emotions and make connections between different events or thoughts and the triggered emotions. The primary purpose of having an emotionally supportive community is to support your little citizens when they have their ups and downs and to coach them on how to effectively function in life without being governed by emotions.

After all, emotions and feelings are real, but they are not intelligent. What? We have become so comfortable with our emotions and feelings that we refer to them as if they were human. It appears that our emotions and feelings have had such a strong influence over our lives for so long that we consult with our emotions and feelings before making a decision. We all do it at one time or another by making a decision based on how we feel.

You may say, "Sheryl, what does 'keeping the mind occupied' have to do with my little citizens?" A whole lot! Teaching the child at an early age how to avoid being idle minded and not to be ruled by his emotions and feelings is an absolute necessity. Learning this form of control will allow the child to think clearly while fulfilling his purpose in life. The child will be in a favorable position when opportunity knocks, and productivity will become a life-long habit.

The following activities are an excellent source of emotional and social stimulation that will further enhance the development of your little citizens.

## Fill the Atmosphere with Positive Words

One way to stimulate positive thoughts is by playing positive music. After all, music is one of the most effective and universal tools there is, and you can use it anytime throughout the day. Be sure to use music that is filled with words of substance and encouragement; such music will promote pleasant thoughts and productivity throughout the day.

Before the day begins, prepare a CD player or iPod station with a playlist of encouraging music. Make a schedule of the most appropriate time to share these songs. For example, a cheerful song played in the morning will set the tone for the rest of the day. Or, as the little citizens are engaging in various individual activities, play soft music in the background that constantly interjects and reinforces positive and productive thoughts, emotions, and behavior.

*Emotions and feelings are real, but they are not intelligent.*

## Teaming Up

By pairing up the children in teams, this activity addresses the child's social and emotional skills. The child learns the importance of not living a self-centered life, meaning the mind should not always be focused on self. Rather, the mind should be stretched to think about others during their time of need and during their time of celebration. Over time, the children who have been paired together will learn how to be considerate, both sympathetically and empathetically. The emotional connection that is developed by each team will eventually go beyond just the two of them and permeate the entire community. The social benefit of this activity is that it strengthens interpersonal and language development skills. Teaming up can be quite beneficial for those children who are shy and feel more comfortable communicating one-on-one, rather than in a group. Implement this activity during clean up time and/or for special assignments.

Here are some examples of the best and worst combinations to keep in mind when pairing off your little citizens.

**Best: Shy and Outgoing.** A child who is outgoing will become the spokesperson for the shy little citizen, for we all know that it is quite easy to overlook a child who is shy. Also, the child who is more outgoing will become a role model for his shy teammate to emulate. A child may be shy and quiet, relying more heavily on his emotional skills, which heightens his awareness of others. This beautiful combination brings balance to both the shy and outgoing little citizens, both socially and emotionally.

The only drawback to this combination is that you do not want the shy little citizen to become dependent on the outgoing child, so I encourage you to challenge the shy one to take the lead during events that require them to work as a team.

**Worst: Outgoing and Outgoing.** This is not a good combination from the standpoint that both members will constantly be in competition will each other because they both have advanced social skills, thereby hindering each other from being good listeners and being sensitive to one another's needs.

## Get a Job

Putting everyone to work by creating jobs/duties that are centered around the daily operations of the community will not only productively preoccupy the mind of your citizens, helping them maintain positive emotions and increasing productivity within the community, but it will also help manage the negative (i.e., physical aggression, oppositional defiance, angry outbursts, etc.) behavior that oftentimes disrupts the flow of the community.

It is essential for your little citizens to be familiar with good work ethics at an early age. Then, when they do become of age and eventually enter into the workplace, the foundation has already been laid for being a responsible, task-oriented employee.

Create jobs/duties appropriate for the functionality of your community. Make sure the jobs/duties are developed around transitions and/or class assignments. For example, if one of the transitions during the day is lining up to go outside or to go to lunch, then you create a job title, such as a line monitor, and appoint a little citizen to make sure everyone is present in line.

Develop a systematic method in which the little citizens can easily understand how to find their names, job title/position, and the shift they are to work. I would recommend using colorful objects (i.e., Velcro, markers, colorful bands) to symbolically represent the jobs/duties and the time the shift starts. For example, if the red dot is behind Carlos's name, he automatically knows that his job for today is helping to set the table for lunch around noon. **Note:** Always rotate jobs so that the little citizens get an opportunity to experience each position.

# Reflections

# Reflections

# Chapter 14

## Brushes and Combs: Emotionally Different

Any time you expound upon the emotional differences between girls and boys, one chapter is not enough. Truly, it would take an entire book to provide the detail needed to completely understand these differences and how to properly respond to our little citizens accordingly. So let this chapter be considered as a quick, introductory course on the emotional differences between boys and girls. Let's get started!

### No Generalizations

When developing an emotionally supportive community that meets the requirements of all your members, you will have to take into consideration that everyone is not the same mentally, socially, or emotionally; no two citizens have the same personality. A flourishing community is based on the leader's ability to recognize the differences that exist amongst its members and then interface accordingly. It is definitely not wise to generalize everyone as being emotionally equal because everyone thinks and responds differently to life events, circumstances, and/or challenges.

The uniqueness of your community hinges upon you being open to each child's emotional state, while at the same time providing meaningful and creative activities (i.e., reading a book on emotions during story time, etc.) that will challenge the children to do the following:

- Explore their emotions
- Explore appropriate and inappropriate actions connected with a particular emotion and/or feeling
- Look at the situation from a different perspective
- See themselves mentally responding to a situation in an appropriate manner

In generalizing the emotional state of your citizens, you forfeit the opportunity to learn the unique emotional makeup of the children you oversee. Indeed, it is essential to understand how each child responds in good times and not so good times. Learning the emotional makeup of your community enables you to provide the essential elements they need to feel emotionally secure: love, patience, guidance, encouragement, stability, and support. Children are more psychologically vulnerable than we are as adults; therefore, their emotions and feelings should always be treated with tender, loving care.

## Emotional and Cultural Differences

Let's briefly look at the factors that contribute to the emotional and cultural differences between boys and girls.

Females are "combs," and males are "brushes." Go to your bathroom and pull out a comb and a brush. First, comb your hair from top to bottom. Feel how the comb touches your scalp while you are stroking your hair. The comb is going beyond the surface. Now start brushing your hair. Notice how the brush does not go as deep as the comb. Females can be referred to as combs because they are more sensitive, emotional, and detailed than their male counterparts. Males, on the other hand, are like brushes from the standpoint that they are more broad and general than females. The innate emotional makeup of both boys and girls allows you and I not only to understand why boys and girls think differently, but also why they emotionally connect or disconnect and why they respond differently to situations and events.

*Girls are born with nurturing qualities,*
*but boys are born with provider qualities.*

**Culturally Acceptable:** It is quite obvious that our society has an influence over our emotional makeup. As a result, girls and boys are taught to respond differently when it comes to utilizing emotions. It is culturally acceptable for girls to express themselves emotionally, even to the point of being melodramatic. In contrast, boys are taught to suppress emotions to the point of being silent. Have you ever noticed how boys can emotionally distance themselves from a situation that would normally stir up some kind of emotional response? Instead of expressing feelings, they shrug their shoulders as if saying, "I don't know." These traditional patterns are ingrained into our children at an early age and are neatly packed into their emotional baggage to carry into adulthood.

**Innate Differences:** Being born with innate differences is another reason boys and girls respond to situations differently. There is a list of contributing factors to be discussed in further detail in my next book, *X Boys, Y Girls.* For example, girls are born with nurturing qualities, but boys are born with provider qualities. I believe this helps explain the emotional differences that exist between a boy and girl. These innate qualities are quite apparent, even during playtime. For example, it is socially acceptable for little girls to be seen holding a baby doll, pretending to attend to the doll's emotional and physical needs. And the boys are typically presented with action-packed toys, such as play hammers, drills, guns, dump trucks, fire trucks, and race cars. These innate differences, which one can observe during play, help explain why girls are nurturers by nature and, therefore, more in tune with their emotions and feelings and the feelings and emotions of others. In contrast, boys are innately designed to be providers/leaders; therefore, they are less emotionally sensitive and are, instead, more physically and mentally driven in life. I am not saying boys are entirely emotionless, but they are less emotionally driven than girls. That is why girls are combs, and boys are brushes.

**Conditioned Emotions:** The little citizen's home environment plays a big part in the development of his emotional state. Children emulate their parents behaviorally, mentally, socially, morally, and even emotionally. In other words, children become a reflection of their parents, mirroring how the parent responds emotionally to life events and/or situations—be it negative or positive. These conditioned emotions become the templates used during intrapersonal and interpersonal relationships. **Note:** Leaders, do not get frustrated or become impatient with a child when he is emotionally distressed. Remember, he has been conditioned to think and respond this way, and it is your job to help redirect his thoughts so that he is better equipped to address the situation, as opposed to becoming a prisoner of the situation or his emotions.

## No Nagging or Yelling

Leaders, let it not be part of your nature to nag or yell at your citizens, especially boys. Constant nagging and yelling will not only stifle their developmental growth (socially, emotionally, and mentally), but it will also deplete the emotional support that was originally established for the community. This section is really directed towards women who oversee a community. I indicated earlier that boys are innately designed to be leaders and providers. Anytime a male child is being nagged at or yelled at by a female in authority, they automatically close up emotionally for two reasons:

- Being yelled at or nagged is too emotional for him, making him unwilling or unable to give.
- He feels like what he was innately designed to be, a leader/provider, is being threatened, so he will emotionally and mentally cut himself off from the situation.

*I recall a story of a grandmother riding with her daughter and the daughter's three-year-old son. As the grandmother was sitting in the back of the car with her grandson, the mother disciplined her son by yelling at him. The little boy automatically shut down, both mentally and emotionally, and started talking about what he had learned in school that day. Children are smart!*

*I recommend, ladies, that you recognize the good the child has done first. Then, you can calmly tell him what he needs to do or failed to do, but do not yell or nag because he will walk away emotionally and mentally. Words of wisdom!*

# Reflections

# *Reflections*

# Closing Words

Throughout this book, I have built a strong case for creating an emotionally healthy community. This environment will help your little citizens grow and develop as they explore and operate within their surroundings.

As a people-centered leader, you must place emotional stability on the top of your list. Children can concentrate better when they are not being governed by their out-of-control emotions. After all, unwieldy or inappropriately expressed emotions can distract a little citizen from receiving all his or her community has to offer. In other words, children thrive when they are healthy emotionally and securely connected to their community.

Emotions are real, but not intelligent. Children's emotions were not designed to govern their lives. Rather, emotions can assist them in gaining a better understanding of life experiences and employing empathy towards fellow citizens.

I assure you, if you diligently implement the principles, techniques, and strategies I have presented in this book, your little citizens, over time, will begin to take ownership of their community; they will readjust their thoughts to line up with the mental movie of the community; and they will become what they were destined to become: productive little citizens.

Warmest Regards,
Sheryl L. Brown

# References

McGhee, P.E. *Understanding and Promoting the Development of Children's Humor.* New York: Kendall/Hunt, 2002.

Raghunathan, Raj. "The Need to Be Busy: An Idle Mind Is Not Just Boring, but Also Unhappy," *Psychology Today*, June 14, 2011, https://www.psychologytoday.com/blog/sapient-nature/201106/the-need-be-busy (accessed April 11, 2016).

Solter, Aletha J. *Helping Young Children Flourish. Goleta*, CA: Shining Star Press, 1989.